Ad in Suburbia

Boston Area edition 2003

The guide to outings, activities and enrichment
classes for children 0-14

To

Sam and Jake

This edition covers outings, activities and classes for children 0-14 in the suburban Boston area.

There are 2 sections:
1. ***Outings & Activities*** which list sites for day trip outings and
2. ***Classes*** which list area enrichment classes by topic.

The listings are grouped by activity or subject. Location, contact information, discounts, and other valuable information is included. In the back of the book, there are indexes by town noting activities or classes in that area.

USAGE NOTICE

This book is intended for reference purposes only. It is not meant to list every available option for outings or activities and a listing makes no representation of fitness. The information is current, to the best of our knowledge, as of publication.

Prices, services and programs included in this book are subject to change without notice. It is always a good idea to call ahead and verify information before your outing or activity.

LISTINGS

Listings are for informational purposes. If you know of additional places for outings, or organizations that offer classes, that would like to be listed, please contact us at:

Kiwi Publishing
P.O. Box 493
Hopkinton, MA 01748

Or email us at:
info@adventuresinsuburbia.com

ADDITIONAL COVERAGE AREAS

The following metropolitan areas are covered by our *Adventures in Suburbia* series:

Boston, Providence, Orange County
California, Phoenix, and
Raleigh/Durham

If you are interested in information
on a listed area, please contact us at
orders@adventuresinsuburbia.com

ISBN 0-9743319-0-2

Cover Photograph by Christine Gallagher

GUITE TO ABBREVIATIONS AND TERMS USED IN THIS BOOK

A   Adult (over 18)

S   Senior-generally over
                65, in some cases 62

C   Child – ages listed

MC   Master Card

V   Visa

D   Discover

AMX   American Express

J   January

Ap   April

Jn   June

Ju   July

Sep   September

O   October

Nov   November

Street parking: There may be meters for street parking. It is a good idea to bring coins-usually quarters.

N/A   Not applicable or Not available at time of publication

OUTINGS & ACTIVITIES

Suburban Boston offers many places for great outings and day trips. The category index should help you find what you want.

When planning an outing, remember to call ahead to confirm hours of operation and any seasonal restrictions.

Category Index

Amusement Places and Theme Adventures

Northern Suburbs

Salem Witch Village

Museum features exhibits on the myths and facts of witchcraft.

Website: www.salemwaxmuseum.com/swv/home.html

Location: 282 R Derby St., Salem

Major Routes/Cross Streets: 114 & 1A/Washington St./New Derby Street.

Parking: Parking garage adjacent to Salem Wax Museum as well as on street parking

Phone: 978-740-2929

Hours: Ap-Jn & S 10-6, Ju & Ag 10-10, O extended hours, N-Mr 11-4 7 days a week, closed holidays

Cost: A$5.50, S$5, C$3, 5 and under FREE

Discounts: Hysteria Pass Discount admission, discount tickets on-line

Credit cards accepted: MC,V,AMX
FREE admission hours: N/A
Food available at site: No
Ages: 0-14
Available for Birthday parties?
N/A
Strollers allowed? YES
Changing station: YES
Notes:_____

Salem 1630: Pioneer Village

Outdoor 17th Century fishing village is re-created and features working blacksmith. Self-guided tours.
Website: www.7gables.org/pv.htm
Location: Forest River Park, off West Avenue
Major Routes/Cross Streets: Rt.114/1A (Lafayette St.)/West
Parking: parking lot
Phone: 978-745-0525 or 978-744-0991
Hours: J & Ag M-Sa 10-5 & Su 12-5, My-Oc10-5 – call to confirm hours
Cost: A$7.50, S$6.50, C$5.50 (5-12), under 5 FREE

Discounts: Senior and AAA, combo ticket with House of 7 Gables
Credit cards accepted: MC, V
FREE admission hours: N/A
Food available at site: Drinks only
Ages: 0-14
Available for Birthday parties? N/A
Strollers allowed? YES
Changing Station: No
Notes:_____

Salem Trolley Tours

1 hour narrated rides aboard Salem Trolley viewing historic sites.
Website: www.salemweb.com/guide/trolley.htm
Location: 8 Central St., Salem
Major Routes/Cross Streets: Pick up trolley at visitors center
Parking: public parking garage
Phone: 978-744-5469
Hours: Ap-O daily 10-5, weekends Mr&Nov weather permitting
Cost: A$10, S$9, C$5 (5-12), under 5 FREE, Family$25 (2A&2C)
Discounts: AAA

Credit cards accepted: MC, V, AMX, D
FREE admission hours: N/A
Food available at site: No
Ages: 0-14
Available for Birthday parties? YES
Strollers allowed? Yes (folded)
Changing station: N/A
Notes: <u>trolley is heated in cooler months but no air conditioning in summer</u>

Old Sturbridge Village

Outdoor village representing early 19th century rural New England life. Village is open year-round and generally takes 3-4 hours to visit.

Website: www.osv.org
Location: 1 Old Sturbridge Village Rd., Sturbridge
Major Routes/Cross Streets: Rt. 90/Rt.20
Parking: Free parking in lots
Phone: 508.347.3362 or 1-800-SEE-1830
Hours: Jan-F 9-4 weekends, O-Jn 9:30am-4pm, closed holidays
Cost: A$20, S$18, C (6-15)$10, under 6 FREE
Discounts: check library for passes
FREE admission hours: Tickets good for 2 consecutive days so day #2 is Free
Credit cards accepted: MC, V, AMX
Food available at site: Tavern restaurant and cafeteria on site. Picnic area also.
Ages: 0-14

Available for Birthday parties?
YES
Strollers allowed? YES
Changing station: YES
Notes: Leashed pets welcome
too_____

The Kid's Place
1000sf 2-room play area with toys, slides, blocks, play kitchen, dress up, puppets and more. Scheduled weekly playgroups.
Website: N/A
Location: 8 Ledgemere Plaza/300 Eliot St., Ashland
Major routes/cross street: Rt.126
Parking: Free parking lot
Phone: 508-881-4414
Hours: Playgroups scheduled 10-5
Cost: $185/per year
Discounts: only $10 for each additional child in playgroup, $25 for each additional playgroup
Credit cards accepted: N/A
FREE admission hours: N/A
Food available at site: NO
Ages: focus age group 0-4

Available for Birthday parties?
YES
Strollers allowed: YES
Changing station: YES
Notes:_____

Breezy Picnic Grounds and Waterslides

Sandy beach at Whitins Reservoir and shady picnic area with lots of tables, snack bar & game room. Beach has certified lifeguards and twisty waterslides.
Website: www.breezypicnicwaterslide.com
Location: 520 Northwest Main Street, Douglas
Major routes/cross streets: I395/Sutton Ave.
Parking: Free Parking lot across street
Phone: 508-476-2664 or 888-821-6222
Hours: Weekends Jn 1-15, then daily through Labor Day.
Waterslides 10-6, park 9:30-6:30
Cost: A$14, C$14(5+), C$8 (2-4), under 2 free

Discounts: AAA
Credit cards accepted: MC,V,D
FREE admission hours: N/A
Food available at site: YES
Ages: 0-14
Available for Birthday parties?
YES
Strollers allowed? YES
Changing station: YES
Notes:_____

<u>Chocolate Factory Tours</u>

See candy being made with samples for all ☺

Where:	Hebert Candies Rt.20 Shrewsbury
Phone:	1-800-642-7702
Website:	www.hebertcandies.com
When:	Tours are Tuesday, Wednesday and Thursday 10:30am-2:30pm
Cost:	Free

Southern Suburbs

Edaville Railroad

Museum, 5.5 mile train ride through 200 acres of cranberry bogs, children's rides, carousel. Fun trains to play on. Train rides every 45 minutes.

Website: www.edaville.org
Location: Off Route 58, Carver
Major Routes/Cross Streets: Rt. 495/Rt.58
Parking: free parking in adjacent lot
Phone: 508-866-8190 or toll free 877-EDAVILLE
Hours: Daily 10:30am – 9pm *some seasonal closing
Cost: A$16, S$16, C$16 (3+) under 3 free, and discounts should include AAA
Discounts: combo tickets
Credit cards accepted: MC, V, AMX, D
FREE admission hours: N/A
Food available at site: YES
Ages:0-12

Available for Birthday parties?
YES
Strollers allowed: YES
Changing station: YES
Notes: <u>all rides are outside and
there are no restrooms on the train.</u>

Plimoth Plantation

Outdoor village representing Pilgrim
life. Live actors interact with visitors
to bring the village to life. A visit will
generally take 3-4 hours.
Website: www.plimoth.org
Location: Plimoth plantation
highway, Plymouth
Major routes/cross streets:
Rt.3A/"Plimoth Plantation Highway"
Parking: Free parking in lot
Phone: 508-746-1622
Hours: Ap-N 9-5 7 days a week,
closed Dec-Mar
Cost: A$22, S$20, C$14 (6-12), 5
and under FREE
Discounts: library passes available
Credit cards accepted: MC,V,D
FREE admission hours: N/A
Food available at site: Yes-
Cafeteria

Ages: 0-14
Available for Birthday parties?
Call
Strollers allowed? YES
Changing station: YES, in visitor
center
Notes: picnic area too_____

Pirate Adventures

1-hour Pirate Adventure excursions
for kids of all ages. Passengers' sail
aboard a "pirate ship" complete with
flag and "cannons". In the harbor,
passengers help reclaim treasure set
in lobster traps.
Website: www.lobstertalesinc.com
www.pirateadventure.com
Location: Town Wharf, Plymouth,
MA
Major routes/cross streets: Rte.
44/Water Street/Town Wharf
Parking: metered parking
Phone: 508-746-5342
Hours: Daily June, July & August,
selected dates April, May,
September and October
Cost: A$12, S$11, C$10 under 4 $8
Discounts: $1 off web coupon

Credit cards accepted: MC, V, AMX, D
FREE admission hours: N/A
Food available at site: NO
Ages: 0-14
Available for Birthday parties? YES
Strollers allowed: NO
Changing station: NO
Notes:_____

Rainy Day Ideas

On rainy days, try some projects at home such as melting old crayons and cutting out new ones with cookie cutters shapes.

For even more creative ideas check out the "Rainy Day Activity Book" *How to make play dough, bubbles, monster repellent and more* by Jennifer Radar.

Historic Sites

Orchard House/Louisa May Alcott's House

Alcott family home-site where Louisa May Alcott wrote *Little Women*. House is shown by 30-minute guided tour. Site also features special events including a writing workshop with published authors for kids 8-12.

Website: www.louisamayalcott.org
Location: 399 Lexington Road, Concord
Major Routes/Cross Streets: 2A/Lexington Rd./Concord Center
Phone: 978-369-4118
Parking: Free parking in the Wayside lot behind the house
Hours: Ap-O 10-4:30 M-Sa, Su 1-4; N-Mr M-F 11-3, Sa 10-4:30, Su 1-4, Closed holidays and Jan 1-15
Cost: A$7, S$6, C$4 (6-17), under 6 FREE, Family$16 (2A & 2C)

Discounts: AAA, WGBH members, MTA, web coupons
Credit cards accepted: MC, V
FREE admission hours: N/A
Food available at site: NO
Ages: 8-14 (ideally of interest to older children)
Strollers allowed: not in the house
Changing station: NO
Notes: no backpacks allowed in the house

Saugus Ironworks National Historic Site

The site of the first integrated ironworks in North America. Site illustrates the importance of ironworks to 17th century settlements. It is mostly outdoors and takes about 2 hours to visit.
Website: www.nps.gov/sair/
Location: 244 Central St., Saugus
Major routes/cross streets: Rt. 1/ Main Street
Parking: Free parking lot
Phone: 781-233-0050
Hours: 9-4
Cost: FREE

Discounts: N/A
Credit cards accepted: N/A
FREE admission hours: ALL
Food available at site: No
Ages: 0-14
Available for Birthday parties?
N/A
Strollers allowed? Yes, but there
are some stairs
Changing station: NO
Notes:_____

Salem Maritime National Historic Site

Site featuring Salem's maritime
history. Ranger led tours available.
Website: www.nps.gov/sama
Location: 174 Derby St., Salem
Major routes/cross streets: Rt.
114
Parking: public parking lot, garages
and street parking
Phone: 508-744-4323
Hours: Daily year round 9-5
Cost: A$5, S$3, C$3(6-10), under 6
FREE, Family $10
Discounts: N/A
Credit cards accepted: N/A

FREE admission hours: N/A
Food available at site: N/A
Ages: all
Available for Birthday parties?
N/A
Strollers allowed? N/A
Changing station: N/A
Notes: <u>tours include Salem's tall
ship "Friendship"</u>

House of Seven Gables
The house that inspired
Hawthorne's 1851 novel holds 6
rooms of period furniture as well as
secret staircases.
Website: www.7gables.org
Location: 54 Turner St., Salem
Major routes/cross streets: Rt.
114/Salem Ctr./Derby St.
Parking: street parking, public lots
and garages
Phone: 978-744-0991
Hours: Nov-June 10-5, July-Oct 10-
7, closed first 3 weeks in January
Cost: A$10, S$9, C$6.50 (5-12),
under 5 FREE

Discounts: combo tickets with Salem Pioneer Village, $1 off web coupon, members free
Credit cards accepted: MC, V
FREE admission hours: N/A
Food available at site: Yes- Garden Cafe
Ages: 0-14
Available for Birthday parties? N/A
Strollers allowed? Only on grounds, not in the house
Changing station: YES
Notes:_____

Minute Man National Historic Park

Park features historic sites and structures associated with the opening battles of the Revolutionary War. Kids can enjoy hiking, wildlife and daily musket firing demonstrations. Ask about Junior Ranger program.
Website: www.nps.gov/mima/vcenter.htm
Location: 174 Liberty St., Concord

Major routes/cross streets: Rt. 2A/ Rt.4/"Battle road"
Parking: lot off monument road
Phone: 978-369-6993
Hours: Visitor's center open 9-5:30 daily in summer, 9:30-4 in winter, closed holidays
Cost:$3 fee for building, park free
Discounts: N/A
Credit cards accepted: N/A
FREE admission hours: park free
Food available at site: No
Ages: 0-14
Available for Birthday parties? N/A
Strollers allowed? YES
Changing station: YES
Notes: picnics allowed, check out "Bullet house" on monument road where bullet from 1775 battle is still lodged_____**Battle is re-created on Patriot's Day see www.nps.gov/mima-parkevents.

Sleepy Hollow Cemetery
Historic point of interest with graves of Thoreau, Emerson, Hawthorne, Alcotts and others.

Website: N/A
Location: Route 62W, Concord
Major routes/cross streets: Rt. 62
Parking: free parking
Phone: For information call Concord Chamber of Commerce 978-369-0113
Hours: dawn to dusk
Cost: Free
Discounts: N/A
Credit cards accepted: N/A
FREE admission hours: All
Food available at site: No
Ages: 0-14
Available for Birthday parties? N/A
Strollers allowed: YES
Changing station: No
Notes:_____

<u>Plymouth Rock</u>

View the rock, believed to be the boulder upon which the Pilgrims landed in 1620, in Pilgrim Memorial State park.

Website: N/A
Location: water street-waterfront downtown Plymouth near Mayflower II
Major Routes/Cross Streets: water street/Rt.44
Parking: street parking and parking lot
Phone: N/A
Hours: No set hours
Cost: FREE
Discounts: N/A
Credit cards accepted: N/A
FREE admission hours: ALL
Food available at site: NO (but local restaurants and snack shops are available across the street)
Ages: 0-14
Available for Birthday parties? N/A
Strollers allowed? YES

Changing station: NO
Notes:_____

Mayflower II

The Mayflower II is a replica of the pilgrim's ship. Live actors tell stories of the hardships aboard that voyage. At least 1 hour is needed for the visit.

Website: www.plimoth.org/museum/ mayflower/mayflowe.ht
Location: Water Street (on the waterfront), Plymouth
Major Routes/Cross Streets: Rt. 3A
Parking: street parking available
Phone: 508-746-1622
Hours: 9-5
Cost: A\$8, S\$7, C\$6(6-12), under 6 FREE
Discounts: members free
Credit cards accepted: V, MC, D
FREE admission hours: n/a
Food available at site: NO-no food or drink allowed on board
Ages: 0-14

Available for Birthday parties?
N/A
Strollers allowed? Strollers cannot access lower level of ship, no elevator
Changing station: NO
Notes: public bathrooms available

Colonial Lantern Tours
Narrated tour explores the town's historic sites and its changes through the centuries. Outdoor, 1 mile walk carrying candle-lit punched tin lantern.
Website: n/a
Location: 98 Water St., Plymouth
Major routes/cross streets: Rt. 44
Parking: parking lot and street parking
Phone: 508-747-4284 or 800-698-5636
Hours: Memorial Day – Labor Day tours start at 9:30am and run every hour
Cost: call
Discounts: n/a
Credit cards accepted: n/a
FREE admission hours: n/a

Food available at site: NO
Ages: 0-14
Available for Birthday parties?
N/a
Strollers allowed? YES
Changing station: NO
Notes:_____

<u>Sail aboard a sloop as it was in 1900</u>.

Where: Sail from "T" wharf in Rockport

When: 3 trips daily

Phone: 978-546-9876

Museums

Children's Discovery Museum

Actually 2 museums: Children's Discovery Museum focuses on toddlers and preschool children but the Science Discovery Museum focuses on school age children.

Website: www.discoverymuseums.org

Location: 177 Main Street, Acton

Major routes/cross streets: Rt. 27/ Rt.2

Parking: free parking in lot

Phone: 978-264-4200

Hours:
Children's Discovery museum: W,Th,Sa&Su 9-4:30, T&F 1-4:30
Science Discovery Museum: T,Th,F 1-4:30, W1-6, Sa&Su 9-4:30

Cost: 1 museum: A$8, S$7, C$8, under 1 FREE. Both museums: A$12, S$11, C$12 under 1 free

Discounts: members free, check library for passes

Credit cards accepted: AMX, MC, V
FREE admission hours: N/A
Food available at site: NO
Ages: 0-14
Available for Birthday parties?
YES
Strollers allowed? YES
Changing station: YES
Notes:_____

DeCordova Museum and Sculpture Park

Interactive art experience for kids. Focus on American contemporary and modern artists. Galleries, exhibits and educational programs for families introduces children to museums. Tours available. Check out free family programs on the 1st Sunday of each month. Outdoor sculpture park too.
Website: www.decordova.org
Location: 51 Sandy Pond Road, Lincoln
Major routes/cross streets: Rt.2/Rt.126/Baker Bridge Road
Parking: parking lot
Phone: 781-259-8355

Hours: T-Sun 11-5 and selected Monday Holidays. Sculpture park open year-round during daylight hours.
Cost: A$6, S$4, C$4 (6-12), under 6 FREE
Sculpture park is FREE
Discounts: members, AAA, WGBH
Credit cards accepted: V, MC
FREE admission hours: ALL at Sculpture Park
Food available at site: YES
Ages: 0-14
Available for Birthday parties?
Rooms available for rent
Strollers allowed? YES
Changing station: YES
Notes: if child likes to draw, pack a sketchbook. Also, picnics allowed in sculpture park

Jeremiah Lee Mansion & JOJ Frost Folk Art Museum

Georgian mansion with 18th century furnishings & the Frost Folk Art museum featuring scenes of life in Marblehead, fishermen, mariners and families.

Website: none
Location: 170 Washington St., Marblehead
Major routes/cross streets: Pleasant St./Rt.114/ Rt. 129
Parking: street parking
Phone: 781-631-1768
Hours: Frost museum T-Sa 10-4, Su 1-4, year-round. Mansion June 1-Oct 15 only-closed Nov-May
Cost: Frost museum: Free. Mansion A$5, S$4.50, C$4
Discounts: N/A
Credit cards accepted: not for admission, gift shop only
FREE admission hours: All at Frost
Food available at site: NO
Ages: 8-14
Available for Birthday parties? No
Strollers allowed? Not in house
Changing station: No
Notes:_____

Salem Wax Museum of Witches and Seafarers'

Wax figures bring Salem Witch Trials of 1629 and the adventures of seafarers to life. Exhibit includes a

Dungeon and a Gravestone Rubbing station.

Website: www.salemwaxmuseum.com

Location: 288 Derby St., Salem

Major routes/cross streets: Rt. 1A

Parking: street parking and public lots

Phone: 978-740-2929

Hours: Su-Sa 9-6 in the summer, 11-4 in the winter

Cost: A$5.50, S$5, C$3

Discounts: group discounts available, Hysteria Pass, AAA

Credit cards accepted: V, MC, D

FREE admission hours: N/A

Food available at site: No

Ages: 0-14

Available for Birthday parties? N/A

Strollers allowed? YES

Changing station: N/A

Notes: some scenes can be scary for younger children

New England Pirate Museum

Explore a full-length Pirate ship and an 80-foot cave. Site also features artifacts from sunken ships and pirate treasures. Guided tours.

Website: www.piratemuseum.com
Location: 274 Derby St., Salem
Major routes/cross streets: on the waterfront across from Pickering Wharf.
Parking: street parking and public parking lots
Phone: 978-741-2800
Hours: May-O 10-5 Daily, weekends in November
Cost: A$6, S$5 C$4 (under 14)
Discounts: combo tickets with Witch Dungeon museum and Witch history museum available
Credit cards accepted: MC, V
FREE admission hours: N/A
Food available at site: No
Ages: 0-14
Available for Birthday parties? No
Strollers allowed? Yes, but Museum has stairs
Changing station: No

Notes: <u>air conditioned</u>

Witch Dungeon Museum
Live re-enactment of the trial of Sara Good. Also, guided tour of the dungeon.
Website: www.witchdungeon.com
Location: 16 Lynde St., Salem
Major routes/cross streets: Rt. 107/Rt. 114/North Summer St.
Parking: street parking and lots
Phone: 978-741-3570
Hours: Ap-Nov 10-5
Cost: A$6, S$5, C$4 (4-13) under 4 FREE
Discounts: combo tickets with Pirate museum and witch history museum
Credit cards accepted: MC, V
FREE admission hours: N/A
Food available at site: No
Ages: 0-14
Available for Birthday parties? No
Strollers allowed? Yes, but museum has stairs
Changing station: No
Notes:_____

Wenham Museum

Site includes the 1660 Clafin-Richards house with original furnishings. There are also interactive children exhibits and an antique train room.

Website: www.wenhammuseum.org
Location: 132 Main St., Wenham
Major routes/cross streets: Rt.1A/ Arbor Street
Parking: parking lot
Phone: 978-468-2377
Hours: T-Su 10-4
Cost: A$5, S$4, C$3 (2-17) under 2 free
Discounts: members
Credit cards accepted: AMX, MC, V
FREE admission hours: N/A
Food available at site: no food or drink allowed
Ages: all
Available for Birthday parties? N/A
Strollers allowed? YES
Changing station: YES
Notes:_____

Hammond Castle Museum

Medieval style castle filled with Roman, medieval and Renaissance artifacts. Guided tours of various lengths and topics available. Student groups can even book an overnight visit to the castle.

Website: www.hammondcastle.org
Location: 80 Hesperus Ave., Gloucester
Major routes/cross streets: Rt. 128/Rt. 133E/ Rt.127S
Parking: very limited on site parking
Phone: 978-283-7673
Hours: May-Oct daily 10-5, weekends only Nov-Ap 10-3
Cost: A$8, S$6, C$5 (4-12) under 4 FREE
Discounts: n/a
Credit cards accepted: MC, V
FREE admission hours: none
Food available at site: No
Ages: 0-14
Available for Birthday parties? call
Strollers allowed? YES but on grounds only
Changing station: N/A

Notes: <u>not wheelchair accessible.</u>
<u>Available for overnight visits for</u>
<u>groups of 20 or more</u>

The Essex Shipbuilding Museum

Collection of rare shipbuilding
artifacts including photos, tools,
documents and models. The
riverfront is museum shipyard and
exhibits are housed in the historic
Essex Central School House. Site
also has old cemetery with graves of
veterans from French and Indian
War, Revolutionary War and the
Civil War.

Website:
www.essexshipbuildingmuseum.org
Location: 66 & 28 Main St., Essex
Major routes/cross streets: Rt.
133/ Rt.22
Parking: parking lot
Phone: 978-768-7541
Hours: W & Sa 12-4
Cost: A$4, S$3, C$2.50 (6-12)
under 6 free
Discounts: None
Credit cards accepted: V, MC
FREE admission hours: N/A

Food available at site: No
Ages: 6+
Available for Birthday parties?
N/A
Strollers allowed? Yes
Changing station: No
Notes: includes tour of boat

Whistler House Museum of Art

Site is the birthplace of artist James Abbott McNeil Whistler. The collection includes late 19th and early 20th century American art with an emphasis on New England.
Website: www.whistlerhouse.org
Location: 243 Worthen St., Lowell (in Lowell's historic district)
Major routes/cross streets: Rt.495/Lowell Connector/Thorndike Street/Market Street
Parking: street parking and metered public lots
Phone: 978-452-7641
Hours: W-Su 11-4
Cost: A$5, S$4, C$4
Discounts: AAA, WGBH, members
Credit cards accepted: MC, V
FREE admission hours: N/A

Food available at site: No
Ages: 8-14
Available for Birthday parties? NO
Strollers allowed? No
Changing Station: N/A
Notes:_____

New England Quilt Museum

Exhibits of contemporary, traditional and antique quilts. Programs, workshops, classes and lectures also available.
Website: www.nequiltmuseum.org
Location: 18 Shattuck St. Lowell
Major route/cross streets: Lowell connector/Thorndike St/Dutton St/Market St
Parking: municipal garage on market street 1 block from museum, metered street parking, on weekends lot behind museum is free
Phone: 978-452-4207
Hours: J-A T-S 10-4, M-D T-S 10-4 & S 12-4 closed Mondays
Cost: A$5, S$4, C$4,
Discounts: members free, WGBH 2 for 1

Credit cards accepted: no credit cards for admission
FREE admission hours: None
Food available at site: No
Ages: 0-14
Available for Birthday parties? N/A
Strollers allowed? Yes
Changing station: No
Notes: _ask about scavenger hunt for school-age children_

Peabody Essex Museum
Founded in 1799, it is the oldest continually operating museum in the country. Tour gallery collection and historic homes including Ropes mansion and witch trials.
Website: www.pem.org
Location: East India Square, Salem
Major routes/cross streets: Cross St./Rt. 114E
Parking: Free parking in Liberty St. & South Harbor garages as well as several public lots
Phone: 508-745-1876 or 800-745-4054

Hours: M-Sa 10-5, Su 12-5 Ap-O, T-Sa 10-5, Su 12-5 Nov-March
Cost: A$5, S$4, under 16 FREE
Discounts: members and Salem residents FREE
Credit cards accepted: V, MC, AMX
FREE admission hours: Opening Day June 21, 2003
Food available at site: 2 cafes
Ages: 0-14
Available for Birthday parties? Private parties available
Strollers allowed? YES
Changing station: Yes
Notes:_____

Salem Witch Museum
Museum illustrates the history of the Salem Witch Trials with life size figures. Presentations every 30 minutes.
Website: www.salemwitchmuseum.com
Location: Washington Square, Salem
Major routes/cross streets: Rt.1 (Hawthorne St.)/town common

Parking: street parking or public lots

Phone: 978-744-1692

Hours: Daily 10-5, closed holidays

Cost: A$6, S$5.50, C$4

Discounts: N/A

Credit cards accepted: Not for admission, gift shop only

FREE admission hours: None

Food available at site: No

Ages: 0-14

Available for Birthday parties? N/A

Strollers allowed? Yes

Changing station: Yes

Notes: Much of the exhibit involves dark areas.

Spellman Museum of Stamps and Postal History

Self-guided stamp and postal exhibits with activity center including geography and art projects. Stamp hunts too.
Website: www.spellman.org
Location: 235 Wellesley St. (At Regis College), Weston
Major routes/cross streets: Rt. 30/ Wellesley St.
Parking: parking lot or street parking, no pass required
Phone: 781-768-8367
Hours: Th-Su 12-5, closed selected holiday weekends
Cost: A$5, S$3, under 16 FREE
Discounts: AAA
Credit cards accepted: MC, V, D
FREE admission hours: N/A
Food available at site: No
Ages: 0-14
Available for Birthday parties? Space available for rent
Strollers allowed? Yes

Changing station: Yes
Notes:_____

Charles River Museum of Industry

Museum features history of industry and technology. Story of the American Industrial Revolution is highlighted showcasing: machine tools, watches, steam engines, and textile mill equipment.

Website: www.crmi.org
Location: 154 Moody Street, Waltham
Major routes/cross streets: Rt.20/ Main St./ Moody St.
Parking: municipal lot "Embassy Municipal Parking lot"
Phone: 781-893-5410
Hours: M-Sa 10-5
Cost: A$4, S$2, C$2
Discounts: AAA
Credit cards accepted: None
FREE admission hours: N/A
Food available at site: No food
Ages: all
Available for Birthday parties? N/A
Strollers allowed? Yes

Changing station: Yes
Notes:_____

<u>Danforth Museum of Art</u>
Museum features a junior gallery designed for families as well as exhibits of American Art. Guided tours, artist lectures, workshops and classes also offered.
Website: www.danforthmuseum.org
Location: 123 Union Ave., Framingham
Major routes/cross streets: Rt. 126/Union Ave.
Parking: Free parking lot
Phone: 508-620-0050
Hours: W-Su 12-5
Cost: A$5, S$4, under 12 FREE
Discounts: members free
Credit cards accepted: MC, V
FREE admission hours: N/A
Food available at site: No
Ages: 0-14
Available for Birthday parties? YES
Strollers allowed? Yes
Changing station: No
Notes:_____

Museum of Transportation

Museum has unique vehicles and historic artifacts including America's oldest collection of automobiles.

Website: www.mot.org
Location: 15 Newton Street, Brookline
Major routes/cross streets: Rt.9/Pond St./Newton St.
Parking: free parking in lot
Phone: 617-522-6547
Hours: T-Su 10-5
Cost: A$5, S$3, C$3 (6-18), under 6 FREE
Discounts: AAA, T-pass, MASS teachers, WGBH
Credit cards accepted: MC, V, AMX
FREE admission hours: N/A
Food available at site: No
Ages: 0-14
Available for Birthday parties? Call
Strollers allowed? Yes
Changing station: Yes
Notes:_____

Rose Art Museum

Museum of modern and contemporary art located on Brandeis University campus. Guided tours available Tuesday at 1pm and Wednesday at 3pm

Website: www.brandeis.edu/rose

Location: Brandeis University, 415 South St., Waltham

Major routes/cross streets: Rt. 30

Parking: need Brandeis pass available at public safety booth at main entrance. Pass is free. Park in lot H past museum on left.

Phone: 781-736-3434

Hours: T-Su 12-5 – closed Mondays

Cost: A$3, under 16 FREE

Discounts: members of museum or Brandeis

Credit cards accepted: none

FREE admission hours: none

Food available at site: 2 restaurants on campus

Ages: 0-14

Available for Birthday parties? No

Strollers allowed? Yes

Changing station: No

Notes:_____

Blue Hills Trailside Museum

Indoor and outdoor exhibits. Indoor area features wildlife found on the reservation's 150 miles of trails. Outdoor area features live deer, otters, bobcats and foxes.

Website: www.massaudobon.org/
Location: 1904 Canton Ave, Milton
Major routes/cross streets: Rt. 138
Parking: Free parking lot
Phone: 617-333-0690
Hours: W-Su 10-5
Cost: A$3, S$2, C$1.50 (3-12) under 3 FREE
Discounts: members free
Credit cards accepted: MC, V
FREE admission hours: none
Food available at site: none
Ages: 0-14
Available for Birthday parties? YES
Strollers allowed? YES
Changing station: No
Notes:_____

Fuller Art Museum

Many exhibits of arts and crafts. Guided tours available for groups and last about 1 hour. Museum school offers programs for kids.

Website: www.fullermuseum.org
Location: 455 Oak Street, Brockton
Major routes/cross streets: Cross St./ Rt.27/ Oak St.
Parking: free parking in lot
Phone: 508-588-6000
Hours: T-Su 12-5
Cost: A$5, S$3, under 18 FREE
Discounts: members free
Credit cards accepted: MC, V
FREE admission hours: Martin Luther King Day
Food available at site: Yes, Museum cafe
Ages: 0-14
Available for Birthday parties? YES
Strollers allowed? Yes
Changing station: No
Notes:_____

Attleboro Museum/Center for the Arts

Open, 3500sf, gallery full of exhibits. Basement has classes and other programs. Sculpture garden too.

Website: www.attleboromuseum.org
Location: 86 Park St, Attleboro
Major routes/cross streets: Rt. 152/Rt. 123
Parking: Parking in back
Phone: 508-522-2644
Hours: T-S 10-5
Cost: Free- suggested $2 donation
Discounts: N/A
Credit cards accepted: N/A
FREE admission hours: All
Food available at site: no
Ages: 0-14
Available for Birthday parties? N/A
Strollers allowed? N/A
Changing station: N/A
Notes:_____

US Naval Ship Building Museum

Home of the USS Salem CA-139, the only preserved heavy cruiser in the world. Museum even has overnight adventure program.

Website: www.uss-salem.org
Location: 739 Washington Street, Quincy (formerly Fore River Shipyard)
Major routes/cross streets: southern artery/ 3A (Washington St)
Parking: free parking in lot
Phone: 617-479-7900
Hours: Sa & Su 10-4 and by appointment
Cost: A$6, S$4, C$4 (4-12), under 4 FREE
Discounts: Tin Can Sailors, members of US Cruiser Sailors Association, museum members, for crew, active or retired US military
Credit cards accepted: No
FREE admission hours: None
Food available at site: No
Ages: 0-14
Available for Birthday parties? YES

Strollers allowed? Yes but access to ship is very limited
Changing station: No
Notes:_____

Hull Lifesaving Museum

The museum is the custodian of Point Allerton US Life Saving Station preserves the region's lifesaving traditions and maritime culture. Open water rowing programs and races also available.
Website: www.bostonharborheritage.org
Location: 1117 Nantasket Ave., Hull
Major route/cross streets: Rt.3/Spring Street
Parking: free parking in lot
Phone: 617-925-5433
Hours: Sep-June: F, Sa, Su & School vacations 10-4; June-Aug: W-Su 10-4
Cost: A$2, S$1.50 C$0-18 FREE
Discounts: members free
Credit cards accepted: MC, V
FREE admission hours: 1st Saturday of each month

Food available at site: no
Ages: 0-14
Available for Birthday parties?
N/A
Strollers allowed? Yes
Changing station: No
Notes:_____

Pilgrim Hall Museum

Features include a collection of items that once belonged to the Pilgrims as well as Native American artifacts. Guided tours are offered to groups. Special programs for children available.
Website: www.pilgrimhall.org
Location: 75 Court St. (Rt.3A) Plymouth
Major routes/cross streets: Rt. 3A
Parking: Free parking next to museum
Phone: 508-746-1620
Hours: Feb 1-Dec 31 9:30-4:30 daily, closed Jan
Cost: A$5, S$4.50 C$3 (5-17), under 5 Free
Family $15 (2A & 2C)

Discounts: AAA, members FREE, Plymouth residents FREE
Credit cards accepted: MC, V
FREE admission hours: N/A
Food available at site: No
Ages: 0-14
Available for Birthday parties? N/A
Strollers allowed? Yes, but there are stairs
Changing station: No
Notes:_____

New Bedford Whaling Museum

Museum illustrates the history of whaling and conservation issues. There are interactive exhibits for children as well as art exhibits, lectures and family programs.
Website: www.whalingmuseum.org
Location: 18 Johnny Cake Hill, New Bedford
Major routes/cross streets: Rt. 195/Rt. 18
Parking: Street parking and garage on Elm Street
Phone: 508-997-0046

Hours: 9am-5pm daily, until 9pm 2nd Thursday of each month
Cost: A\$8, S\$7, C\$6 (6-14) under 6 free
Discounts: members
Credit cards accepted: N/A
FREE admission hours: Wednesday afternoons 1-5 – call to confirm
Food available at site: N/A
Ages: 0-14
Available for Birthday parties? N/A
Strollers allowed? N/A
Changing station: N/A
Notes:_____

Battleship Cove

Explore submarine, destroyer and PT boats. Board the battleship USS Massachusetts. Guided tours of the Hiddensee, all others self-guided
Website: www.battleshipcove.org
Location: Battleship Cove, Fall River
Major routes/cross streets: Rt.24/Rt79/Davol St
Parking: free parking in lot

Phone: 508-678-1110 or 1-800-533-3194
Hours: Ap-Jn 9-5 daily, July-Labor Day 9-5:30, Labor Day-Ap 9-4:30
Cost: A$10, S$8, C$5(6-14), under 6 FREE
Discounts: members, AAA, military in uniform FREE
Credit cards accepted: MC, V, D, AMX
FREE admission hours: N/A
Food available at site: YES- snack bar
Ages: 0-14
Available for Birthday parties? YES
Strollers allowed? Yes but cannot bring strollers on board ship
Changing station: No
Notes: _Overnights on board ship available for children 6 years and older_

Children's Museum of Easton

Children's museum with exhibits which include: wood workshop with real tools, art area, "hospital" room, camping and even and old fishing boat.

Website: www.charityadvantage.com/childrensmuseumeaston/home

Location: 9 Sullivan Ave., Easton

Major routes/cross streets: Main street/Center street

Parking: Free parking in lot

Phone: 508-230-3789

Hours: T-Sa 10-5, Su 12-5

Cost: $4.50 per person, under 1 FREE

Discounts: members free

Credit cards accepted: MC, V, D

FREE admission hours: none

Food available at site: No

Ages: 0-10

Available for Birthday parties? YES

Strollers allowed? YES

Changing station: yes

Notes:_____

Marine Museum at Fall River

Museum features world's largest Titanic exhibit as well as exhibit of the Andrea Doria. There is also a display of the Fall River Line artifacts, 150 scale models and 30,000 photos.

Website: www.marinemuseum.org
Location: 70 Water St., Fall River Battleship Cove
Major routes/cross streets: Rt.24/ Rt. 79/ Battleship Cove
Parking: street parking ad parking lot at visitor's center a short distance away
Phone: 508-674-3533
Hours: M-F 9-5, Sa 12-5, Su 12-4
Cost: A$5, S$5, C$4 (5-12) under 5 FREE
Discounts: AAA
Credit cards accepted: N/A
FREE admission hours: N/A
Food available at site: No
Ages: 0-14
Strollers allowed: Yes
Changing station: No
Notes:_____

New Bedford Fire Museum

Collection of antique fire equipment on display in Old Station No.4. Museum collection also includes antique records, fire uniforms, pumps & poles.

Website: www.ci.new-bedford.ma.us/PSAFETY/FIRE/museum.htm

Location: 51 Bedford St., New Bedford

Major routes/cross streets: Bedford St. and corner of 6th St.

Parking: street parking

Phone: 508-992-2162

Hours: Jn & Aug 9-4 daily

Cost: $2

Discounts: members free

Credit cards accepted: N/A

FREE admission hours: N/A

Food available at site: N/A

Ages: 0-14

Available for Birthday parties? N/A

Strollers allowed? N/A

Changing station: N/A

Notes:_____

Nature & Animals

Northern Suburbs

Stone Zoo

Zoo animals include: monkeys, cougars, coyotes, jaguars, leopards, llamas, lemurs and others. There is a barnyard where children can pet goats and sheep.

Website: www.zoonewengland.org
Location: 149 Pond Street, Stoneham
Major Routes/Cross Streets: I93
Parking: free parking in lot
Phone: 781-438-5100
Hours: Summer (April-September) 10-5 daily, weekends 10-6. Winter (October-March) 10-4 daily.
Cost: A$6, S$5, C$4 (2-15), under 2 FREE
Discounts: WGBH, MTA, and coupons
Credit cards accepted: MC, V, AMX
FREE admission hours: N/A
Food available at site: Yes, Safari Grill

Ages: 0-14
Available for Birthday parties? No
Strollers allowed: Yes
Changing station: Yes
Notes:_____

Habitat Education Center and Wildlife Sanctuary

Located on a former estate, this sanctuary offers nature walks, gardens and wildlife. Children may see crayfish, painted turtles, bullfrogs and screech owls.
Website: www.massaudubon.org
Location: 10 Juniper Road, Belmont
Major Routes/Cross Streets: Rt.2/Rt. 60/Clifton St.
Parking: parking lot
Phone: 617-489-5050
Hours: Nature Center: M-F 8-4, S&S 10-4
Trails are open dawn to dusk
Cost: A$4, S$3, C$3 (3-12), under 3 FREE
Discounts: members free
Credit cards accepted: MC, V
FREE admission hours: N/A

Food available at site: snack tray only
Ages: 0-14
Available for Birthday parties? N/A
Strollers allowed: Yes but trails may be rugged
Changing station: No
Notes: _Bathrooms located in the main house_____

The Butterfly Place
Hundreds of butterflies from around the world fly around you as you walk through the indoor sanctuary. Watch the butterflies feed and lay eggs. Children can identify the different types of butterflies using a guide.
Website: www.butterflyplace-ma.com
Location: 120 Tyngsboro Street, Westford
Major Routes/Cross Streets: Rt.495/ Rt.40
Parking: Free parking in lot
Phone: 978-392-0955

Hours: March 1-Columbus Day 10-5 daily
Cost: A$7, S$6, C$5.50 (3-12), 2 and under FREE
Discounts: MTA, WGBH, Museum of Science
Credit cards accepted: MC, V
FREE admission hours: N/A
Food available at site: NO
Ages: 0-14
Available for Birthday parties? Yes
Strollers allowed: YES
Changing station: Yes
Notes: children under 3 must be in a stroller, backpack or carried. Observation room is air conditioned-butterfly atrium is maintained at 80 degrees.

Davis Farm/Davis Mega Maze

Davis Farm is a working farm full of farm animals children can feed and brush. There are rare animals like Kerry cattle, playful Jacob sheep, and Highland cattle. The hayride around the farm is always a treat. Pony rides are available for an additional fee. There is also a playground, water play area, shaded picnic tables and snack stand. Trivia- Mary's house and school (from Mary Had A Little Lamb) were originally located on this farm. The Mega Maze is right across the street from the farm. It is a life-size 3-D game with over 3 miles of pathways.

Website: www.davisfarmland.com

Location: 142 Redstone Hill, Sterling MA

Major Routes/Cross Streets: Rt. 12/ Rt.62

Parking: Free parking in lot

Phone:

Farm   (978)-422-MOOO (6666)

Megamaze   (978) 422-8888

Hours: April-September 9-4:30 daily

Cost: ages 2-60 $11.95, Under 2 FREE

Discounts: members, AAA, coupons

Credit cards accepted: V, MC, D, AMX

FREE admission hours: N/A

Food available at site: YES

Ages:0-8

Available for Birthday parties? YES

Strollers allowed? Yes
Changing station: YES
Notes: <u>new water play area-towels and "swimmer" diapers available at guest services for nominal fee</u>

Wolf Hollow

Learn about wolves in the wild. The Gray Wolf is featured here, as well as Timberwolves and other wolves.
Website:
<u>www.wolfhollowipswich.org</u>
Location: Rt. 133 East, Ipswich
Major Routes/Cross Streets:
Rt.133
Parking: free parking in lot
Phone: 978-356-0216
Hours: Sa & Su weather permitting with presentations at 1:30pm and 3:30pm – call to confirm
Cost: A$5, S$4, C$3.50 (3-17) under 3 FREE
Discounts: none
Credit cards accepted: MC, V
FREE admission hours: None
Food available at site: No
Ages:5-14
Available for Birthday parties? No

Strollers allowed? Yes
Changing station: No
Notes: <u>Group visits welcome during the week, NOTE- this is a natural environment and wolves may eat in view</u>_____

<u>Drumlin Farm Education Center and Wildlife Sanctuary</u>

See owls & birds, maple sugaring, sheep sheering or take nature walks/hikes.
Website: www.lincoln-ma.com/town_groups/drumlin.htm
Location: 208 South Great Road, Lincoln
Major Routes/Cross Streets: Rt.117
Phone: 781-259-9807
Parking: free parking in lot
Hours: Nature Center open March-October T-Su 9-5, November-February T-Su 9-4. Trails keep same hours as Nature Center.
Cost: A$6, S$4, C$4 (3-12), under 3 Free
Discounts: members
Credit cards accepted: MC, V

FREE admission hours: none
Food available at site: juice and snacks only
Ages: 0-14
Available for Birthday parties? No
Strollers allowed? Yes
Changing station: No
Notes:_____

Southwick Zoo

Zoo features animals including lions and tigers. In addition, there is also a play area, elephant and camel rides, and live animal shows. For a lunch break there is a picnic area and snack stand.

Website: www.southwickszoo.com
Location: Rt. 16, Mendon
Major Routes/Cross Streets: Rt. 16
Parking: Free parking in lot
Phone: 800-258-9182
Hours: 10-5 in season April-October
Cost: A$13.75, S$9.75, C$9.75 (3-12) under 3 Free
Discounts: coupons available on-line at the zoo's website, AAA, Family Fun Pass for 12 admissions $90
Credit cards accepted: V, MC, D, AMX
FREE admission hours: N/A
Food available at site: YES
Ages: 0-14

Available for Birthday parties?
YES
Strollers allowed: YES
Changing station: N/A
Notes:_ unique deer forest where
children can hand feed deer

Tower Hill Botanical Gardens

Hike on woodland trails or explore
gardens. Unique gardens include;
'cottage', 'secret' and 'wildlife'
gardens.
Website: www.towerhillbg.org
Location:11 French Dr., Boylston
Major Routes/Cross Streets:
Rt.495/Rt.20
Parking: Free parking in lot
Phone: 508-869-6111 x24
Hours: T-Su 10-5
Cost: A$8, S$5, C$5 (6-18) under 6
FREE
Discounts: members free
Credit cards accepted: MC, V,
AMX, D
FREE admission hours: N/A
Food available at site: YES- cafe
Ages:0-14

Available for Birthday parties?
Available for rental
Strollers allowed? Yes
Changing station: Yes
Notes: Restrooms available. Also, after 4:30 pm on Wednesdays in May through August, admission is ½ price until 8pm.

Marino Lookout farm

Pick your own apples, Asian pears, peaches, and nectarines. Ride a train around the farm. See the petting zoo and bee observatory. Kids club events such as 'Halloween Harvest Day'. During Christmas season there is a farm-Santa, reindeer, and caroling.
Website: www.lookoutfarm.com
Location: 84 Pleasant St., South Natick
Major Routes/Cross Streets: Rt. 16
Parking: free parking in lot
Phone: 508-655-4294
Hours: 10-4 (Market open 7 days 8am-8pm) U Pick starts in August

Cost: A$5, S$5, C$4 (4-12), under 4 FREE
Discounts: N/A
Credit cards accepted: MC, V
FREE admission hours: N/A
Food available at site: only on weekends
Ages: 0-14
Available for Birthday parties? YES. April –August only though.
Strollers allowed: YES
Changing station: No
Notes: farmer's market coupon available at website, Bathrooms are "handi-houses"

Natick Community Organic Farm

Working organic farm with animals and even a maple sugar house. Visitors can help with farm activities. See baby animals (sheep & goats) in season.
Website: www.natickfarm.org
Location: 117 Elliot St (Rte 16), Natick
Major Routes/Cross Streets: Rt.16
Parking: Free parking lot
Phone: 508-655-2204

Hours: M-F 9-5 and during chores on Sa & Su.
Cost: $2 suggested donation
Discounts: N/A
Credit cards accepted: N/A
FREE admission hours: N/A
Food available at site: farm stand
Ages: 0-14
Available for Birthday parties? N/A
Strollers allowed? Yes
Changing station: No
Notes: <u>Autumn Harvest Festival. Maple Syrup collecting.</u>

Lil Folk Farm
Small farm with animals and activities for children.
Website: www.lilfolkfarm.com
Location: 1070 Washington St., Holliston
Major Routes/Cross Streets: Rt.16/Rt.126
Parking: free parking in lot
Phone: 508-429-1700
Hours: only public hours are Friday mornings-$10 per child for animal

visit, snack and craft 9:30-11:30am.
Call for additional times.
Cost: varies
Discounts: N/A
Credit cards accepted: N/A
FREE admission hours: N/A
Food available at site: N/A
Ages: 0-10
Available for Birthday parties?
YES
Strollers allowed: Yes
Changing Station: No
Notes: available for group outings-
playgroups etc.

Garden in the Woods
Explore walking trails through a
wildflower garden with over 1600
types of plants. Informal guided
tours are available at 10am
weekdays and 2pm Sundays. A self-
guided booklet is also available.
Website: www.newfs.org
Location: 180 Hemenway Rd.,
Framingham
Major Routes/Cross Streets: Rt.20
Parking: parking lot
Phone: 508-877-7630

Hours: Ap-Ju 9-7 daily, Ju-Oc T-Su 9-5
Cost: A$7, S$5, C$3 (6-18) under 6 FREE
Discounts: members
Credit cards accepted: MC, V
FREE admission hours: N/A
Food available at site: No
Ages: 0-14
Available for Birthday parties? No
Strollers allowed: Yes but terrain is rugged
Changing station: No
Notes: _Picnic area and restrooms available_

Broadmoor Wildlife Sanctuary

Explore fields, woodlands and wetlands. There are 9 miles of walking trails. Wildlife include: birds, beavers, otters, and ducks.
Website: www.massaudubon.org
Location: 280 Eliot Street, Natick
Major Routes/Cross Streets: Rt. 27/Rt.16
Parking: free parking in lot
Phone: 617-235-3929

Hours: Nature Center T-F 9-5, S&S 10-5
Trails T-Su Dawn-Dusk
Cost: A$4, S$3, C$3 (3-12), under 3 FREE
Discounts: members free
Credit cards accepted: MC, V
Free admission hours: None
Food available at site: No
Ages: 0-14
Available for parties: N/A
Strollers allowed: Yes
Changing station: No
Notes: Backpacks may be easier on trails than strollers

Great Meadows Natural Wildlife Sanctuary
Explore 3000 acres along the Concord and Sudbury rivers. Observe wildlife including various water birds.
Website: http://www.massaudubon.org/Birds_&_Beyond/IBA/sites/iba_greatmeadows.html
Location: Weir Hill Road, Sudbury
Major Routes/Cross Streets: Rt.62

Phone: 617-235-3929
Parking: free parking lot
Hours: 7:30-4:00
Cost: free
Discounts: n/a
Credit cards accepted: n/a
FREE admission hours: all
Food available at site: no
Ages:0-14
Available for Birthday parties? no
Strollers allowed: yes
Changing Station: no
Notes: __picnic area and restrooms are available_____

Stony Brook Reservation

Explore Teal marsh on a series of boardwalks. Observe wildlife including great blue herons, turtles, fish, muskrats, wood ducks, and Canadian geese. Events include wildlife exhibits, guided walks and a Fall Fair.
Website: www.massaudubon.org/nature_connection/sanctuaries/stony_brook/index.html
Location: 108 North Street, Norfolk

Major Routes/Cross Streets:
Rt.1A/Rt.115
Phone: 508-528-3140
Parking: free parking in lot
Hours: Nature Center T-F 9-5, Sa &
Su 10-4 (summer Ju-Ag M 9-5 also)
Trails open dawn to dusk
Cost:A$4, S$3, C$3 (3-12), under 3
FREE
Discounts: members
Credit cards accepted: MC, V
FREE admission hours: Earth Day
Food available at site: Available at
Nature Center T-F 9-5, S&S 10-4
Ages: 0-14
Available for Birthday parties?
YES
Strollers allowed: Yes
Changing Station: Yes
Notes: _restrooms available

South Shore Natural Science Center

Center with indoor and outdoor activity areas focused on environmental education. Explore trails, wildlife habitats and view wildlife.

Website: www.ssnsc.org
Location: Jacobs Lane, Norwell
Major Routes/Cross Streets: Rt.3/Rt.123
Parking: free parking in lot
Phone: 781-659-2559
Hours: M-Sa 9:30-4:30 Closed Sundays
Cost: A$5, S$2.50, C$2.50 (3-15) Under 3 Free
Discounts: members, Massachusetts Federation of Teachers, WGBH, Federated Garden Clubs
Credit cards accepted: MC, V, D
FREE admission hours: admission to Vine Hall Art Gallery, Gift store and trails are all free

Food available at site: snacks only. No food or drink in museum.
Ages:0-14
Available for Birthday parties? YES
Strollers allowed? Yes
Changing station: Yes
Notes: _restrooms in nature center

MDC Blue Hills Reservation & Trailside Museum

Explore 150 miles of trails on the reservation. Museum exhibits feature live deer, otters, foxes and bobcats.
Website: www.massaudubon.org/nature_connection/sanctuaries/blue_hills/index.html
Or
www.state.ma.us/mdc/blue.htm
Location: 1904 Canton Ave., Milton
Major Routes/Cross Streets: Rt. 138
Phone: 617-333-0690
Parking: free parking in lot
Hours: W-Su 10-5, Trails open dawn to dusk daily

Cost: A$3, S$2, C$1.50 (3 - 12)
Discounts: members
Credit cards accepted: MC, V
FREE admission hours: none
Food available at site: none
Ages: 0-14
Available for Birthday parties? Yes
Strollers allowed: Yes
Changing Station: No
Notes:_ Picnic area, restrooms available

Moose Hill Wildlife Sanctuary

Explore almost 2000 acres of grasslands, forests, swamps and bogs. Fun family events include a Halloween Prowl, Summer solstice celebration, hayrides, maple sugaring and scavenger hunts.
Website:
www.massaudubon.org/nature_con nection/sanctuaries/Moose_Hill/ind ex.html
Location: 293 Moose Hill Street, Sharon
Major Routes/Cross Streets: Rt.95/Rt.27
Phone: 617-784-5691

Parking: free parking in lot
Hours: Nature Center open T-Su 9-5, Trails open daily dawn to dusk
Cost: A$3, S$2, C$2 (3-12), under 3 Free
Discounts: members
Credit cards accepted: MC, V
FREE admission hours: none
Food available at site: no
Ages: 0-14
Available for Birthday parties? N/A
Strollers allowed: Yes- but trails may be difficult to navigate
Changing Station: No
Notes: _Restrooms are available

North River
Explore a red maple swamp, cattail marsh and salt marsh. Wildlife may include birds such as scarlet tanagers and even harbor seals.
Website:
http://www.massaudubon.org/Nature_Connection/Sanctuaries/North_River/index.html
Location: 2000 Main St., Marshfield

Major Routes/Cross Streets:
Rt.53/Rt.123/Rt.3A
Phone: 781-837-9400
Parking: parking lot
Ages: 0-14
Hours: Visitor Center M-Sa 8:30-4:30, trails open dawn to dusk daily
Cost: A$4, S$3, C$3 (3-12) under 3 free
Discounts: members free
Credit cards accepted: MC, V
FREE admission hours: none
Food available at site: no
Ages: 0-14
Available for Birthday parties? no
Strollers allowed: yes
Changing Station: no
Notes: <u>summer camp too! Picnic area and restrooms available</u>

Oak Knoll
Hike woodland trails and view wildlife including: cottontail rabbits, woodpeckers, foxes, salamanders and frogs. Guided nature walks are available.
Website:
http://www.massaudubon.org/Nat

ure_Connection/Sanctuaries/Oak_K
noll/
Location: 1417 Park Street,
Attleboro
Major Routes/Cross Streets:
Rt.152/Rt.123
Phone: (508) 223-3060
Parking: parking lot
Hours: Visitor Center T-Sa 10-4,
trails open dawn to dusk daily
Cost: free
Discounts: N/A
Credit cards accepted: N/A
FREE admission hours: all
Food available at site: N/A
Ages: 0-14
Available for Birthday parties?
N/A
Strollers allowed: yes
Changing Station: N/A
Notes: _____

Capron Park Zoo
Zoo with exhibits including snow
leopards and playful otters.
Website:
http://www.capronparkzoo.com

Location: 201 County St., Attleboro
Major Routes/Cross Streets:
Rt.495/Rt.123
Phone: (508) 222-3047
Parking: parking lot
Hours: 10-4
Cost: A$3.50, S$2, C$2 (3-12)
under 2 FREE
Discounts: Attleboro residents ½
price
Credit cards accepted: none
FREE admission hours: none
Food available at site: concession
stand
Ages: 0-14
Available for Birthday parties?
YES
Strollers allowed: yes
Changing Station: N/A
Notes: _____

Parent resources:

www.wahm.com (for work-at-home moms)
www.momsclub.org (for moms)
www.athomedad.com (for at-home dads)
www.mothersandmore.org (for moms)

Orchards

Berlin Orchards

Pick apples in the orchards. See a cider mill on the farm. Weekend hayrides. Animals too.

Website: www.berlinorchards.com
Location: 200 Central Street, Berlin
Major Routes/Cross Streets: Rt.62/Rt.495
Parking: free parking in lot
Phone: 978-838-2400
Hours: 10-6 in season
Cost: depends on fruit amounts
Discounts: N/A
Credit cards accepted: MC, V, D, AMX
FREE admission hours: All- no cost to visit
Food available at site: Yes - restaurant
Ages: 0-14
Available for Birthday parties? No
Strollers allowed? YES
Changing station: No

Notes: <u>also gourmet shop, gift shop.</u>
<u>Strawberry Festival too!</u>

Nashoba Valley Winery and Orchards

Pick your own fruit: raspberries,
plums, apples, peaches and
blackberries.
Website: www.nashobawinery.com
Location: 100 Wanaquadoc Hill Rd.,
Bolton
Major Routes/Cross Streets:
Rt.495/Rt.290/Rt.117
Parking: free parking in lot
Phone: 978-779-5521
Hours: Daily 11-5 in season for
orchard
Cost: no admission fee
Discounts: N/A
Credit cards accepted: MC, V, AMX
FREE admission hours: ALL
Food available at site: YES-
restaurant
Ages: 0-14
Available for Birthday parties? No
Strollers allowed? Yes
Changing station: No

Notes: <u>picnics allowed, restaurants available</u>

Russell Orchards
Pick apples, strawberries, raspberries and blueberries. Hayrides on weekends. Cider pressing and farm animals too.
Website: <u>www.russellorchardsma.com</u>
Location: 143 Argilla Road, Ipswich
Major Routes/Cross Streets: Rt.133 & 1A
Parking: Free parking in lot
Phone: 978-356-5366
Hours: 9-6 in season
Cost: free admission
Discounts: N/A
Credit cards accepted: MC, V
FREE admission hours: all
Food available at site: Store
Ages: 0-14
Available for Birthday parties? YES
Strollers allowed? Strollers are allowed outside
Changing station: No
Notes: <u>restrooms available</u>

Honeypot Hill Orchards

Pick apples, pears and blueberries. Weekend hayrides, hedgemaze, farm animals, and picnic area.

Website: www.honeypothill.com
Location: 144 Sudbury Road, Stow
Major Routes/Cross Streets: Rt.62W
Parking: Free parking in lot
Phone: 978-562-5666
Hours: 11-5 daily in season
Cost: free admission
Discounts: N/A
Credit cards accepted: No
FREE admission hours: all
Food available at site: Bakery goods only
Ages: 0-14
Available for Birthday parties? YES
Strollers allowed? Yes
Changing station: No
Notes: Picnic area. Restrooms available.

Shelburne Farm

Pick apples, peaches and pumpkins. Weekend hayrides. Apple shop too. Picnic areas.

Website: www.shelburnefarm.com
Location: 106 West Acton Rd., Stow
Major Routes/Cross Streets: Rt.2/Rt.117
Parking: Free parking in lot
Phone: 978-897-9287
Hours: daily 9-6 (picking season is late summer to early autumn)
Cost: free admission
Discounts: N/A
Credit cards accepted: MC, V
FREE admission hours: all
Food available at site: Yes
Ages: 0-14
Available for Birthday parties? Yes
Strollers allowed? Yes
Changing station: No
Notes: special events include pony rides, face painting and hay rides during the season

Hyland Orchard and Brewery

Pick apples and peaches. Peach festival in August.

Website: www.hylandbrew.com
Location: 199 Arnold Rd., Sturbridge
Major Routes/Cross Streets: Off Rt.20, W of Sturbridge Village
Parking: free parking in lot
Phone: 508-347-7500
Hours: summer 11:30-5:30 weekends only, September daily
Cost: free admission
Discounts: N/A
Credit cards accepted: MC, V, D, AMX
FREE admission hours: all
Food available at site: snack bar & light fare
Ages: 0-14
Available for Birthday parties? Yes
Strollers allowed? Yes
Changing station: Yes
Notes: _restrooms available

Marino Lookout Farm

Pick apples and Asian pears. Train ride around the farm, pony rides, petting zoo and bee observatory.

Website: www.lookoutfarm.com
Location: 89 Pleasant St., South Natick
Major Routes/Cross Streets: Rt. 16
Parking: free parking in lot
Phone: 508-653-0653
Hours: T-Su 10-4 in season (Market open 7 days a week)
Cost: A$5, S$5, C$4 (4-12) under 4 free
Discounts: N/A
Credit cards accepted: MC, V
FREE admission hours: N/A
Food available at site: only on weekends
Ages: 0-14
Available for Birthday parties? Yes. April-August only.
Strollers allowed? Yes
Changing station: No
Notes: _restrooms are "port-a-potties"_____

Westward Orchards

Pick blueberries, apples, pears and pumpkins.

Website: www.westwardorchards.com

Location: Rt.111, Harvard

Major Routes/Cross Streets: Rt. 111

Parking: Free parking in lot

Phone: 978-456-8363

Hours: 10-6 in season May 1-December 31, closed Tuesdays

Cost: free admission

Discounts: N/A

Credit cards accepted: N/A

FREE admission hours: all

Food available at site: Yes-farmstore

Ages: 0-14

Available for Birthday parties? N/A

Strollers allowed? Yes

Changing station: N/A

Notes:_____

Clearview Farm

Pick your own apples, peaches, raspberries, blueberries, pumpkins & pears.

Website: www.clearviewfarmstand.com

Location: 4 Kendall Hill Rd., Sterling

Major Routes/Cross Streets: Rt.190/Rt.12/Rt.62/Rt.140

Parking: Free parking in lot

Phone: 978-422-6442

Hours: 9-5 M-F, 10-6 Sa & Su in season (open mid-August)

Cost: free admission

Discounts: N/A

Credit cards accepted: No

FREE admission hours: all

Food available at site: Bakery

Ages: 0-14

Available for Birthday parties? Yes

Strollers allowed? Yes

Changing station: No

Notes: _restrooms available

Carlson Orchards

Pick your own peaches, apples, raspberries, blueberries and nectarines. There is even a cider mill.

Website: www.carlsonorchards.com
Location: 115 Oak Hill Rd., Harvard
Major Routes/Cross Streets: Rt.2/Rt.111
Parking: free parking in lot
Phone: 978-456-3916
Hours: 10-5 daily
Cost: no admission fee
Discounts: N/A
Credit cards accepted: MC, V
FREE admission hours: all
Food available at site: desserts only
Ages: 0-14
Available for Birthday parties? No
Strollers allowed? Yes
Changing station: No
Notes: _restrooms are "port-a-potties"_____

<u>Big Apple Orchard</u>

Pick your own blueberries, raspberries and apples.

Website: <u>www.norfolk-county.com/bigapple</u>

Location: 207 Arnold Street, Wrentham

Major Routes/Cross Streets: I495/King Street

Parking: free parking in lot

Phone: 508-384-3055

Hours: 9-6 June to December

Cost: free admission

Discounts: N/A

Credit cards accepted: no

FREE admission hours: all

Food available at site: Bakery

Ages:0-14

Available for Birthday parties? no

Strollers allowed? Yes

Changing station: no

Notes: __restrooms available____

CN Smith Farm

Pick blueberries, raspberries, strawberries, pumpkins and apples!

Website: www.cnsmithfarminc.com

Location: 325 South St., E. Bridgewater

Major Routes/Cross Streets: Rt.26/Rt.106

Parking: free parking in lot

Phone: 508-378-2270

Hours: 9-4 daily

Cost: no admission fee

Discounts: N/A

Credit cards accepted: MC, V, AMX, D

FREE admission hours: all

Food available at site: N/A

Ages: 0-14

Available for Birthday parties? N/A

Strollers allowed? Yes

Changing station: No

Notes: _restrooms available. Strawberry Festival in June

Ward's Berry Farm

Pick your own blueberries, raspberries, pumpkins, peaches and strawberries! Free hayrides to the strawberry patch. In the Spring there is a 4H barn with baby animals.

Website: no
Location: 614 South Main St., Sharon
Major Routes/Cross Streets: I95
Parking: Free parking in lot
Phone: 781-784-3600
Hours: 9-6 daily-closed Wednesdays (Winter T-S 9:30-6) – call to confirm
Cost: no admission fee
Discounts: N/A
Credit cards accepted: MC, V, AMX, D
FREE admission hours: all
Food available at site: Fruit Smoothie bar
Ages: 0-14
Available for Birthday parties? Yes
Strollers allowed? Yes
Changing station: Yes
Notes: restrooms available

Parks & Hiking Trails

Northern Suburbs

Walden Pond State Reservation

Reservation includes 333 acres surrounding Walden Pond and 2280 acres of woods. Activities include hiking, fishing, swimming, and nature walks. The park has a replica of Thoreau's house. Guided walks are available.

Website: www.state.ma.us/dem/parks/waldn.htm

Location: 915 Walden Street (Rte. 126) Concord

Major Routes/Cross Streets: Rt. 126

Parking: parking lot with $5 entrance fee

Phone: 978-369-3254

Hours: 7-7

Cost: $5 per car (season pass available)

Discounts: N/A

Credit cards accepted: no
FREE admission hours: none
Food available at site: ice cream truck
Ages: 0-14
Available for Birthday parties? no
Strollers allowed? Yes
Changing station: no
Notes: <u>The number of visitors is limited- Call in advance. Dogs are NOT allowed.</u> <u>Bathrooms available. Checks accepted.</u>

Wachusett Mountain Ski Area and State Reservation

Explore hiking and walking trails on 3000 acres reservation with 2000 foot summit! There are picnic areas and scenic vistas.
Website: N/A
Location: Wachusett Moutain, Mountain Road, Princeton
Major Routes/Cross Streets: Rt.2/Rt.140
Parking: free parking lot
Phone: 978-464-2987
Hours: dawn - dusk
Cost: free to hike, $2 to drive to top

Discounts: n/a
Credit cards accepted: n/a
FREE admission hours: all for hiking
Food available at site: no
Ages: 0-14
Available for Birthday parties? n/a
Strollers allowed? no
Changing station: no
Notes: _restrooms in visitor's center. Backpacks are easiest on trails.__

Lynn Shore Reservation/Nahant Beach

Walk along 105 acres on the edge of Nahant Bay (1+ miles of open shoreline). Explore tidal pools and flats. Also, public swimming and a tot lot too.
Website: www.state.ma.us/mdc/lynn_sh.htm
Location: 1 Traffic Circle, Lynn
Major Routes/Cross Streets: 1A/Carroll Highway
Parking: Free parking in lot (main lot closed in the winter), but fee charged to park in Long beach lot

May-Sept. Also street parking available.
Phone: 617-727-1397
Hours: Dawn-dusk
Cost: parking fee in summer
Discounts: N/A
Credit cards accepted: N/A
FREE admission hours: All
Food available at site: no
Ages: 0-14
Available for Birthday parties? n/a
Strollers allowed? yes
Changing station: no
Notes:_ restrooms at Nahant beach only, none on reservation_____

Breakheart Reservation
640 acre forest with rocks, 2 freshwater lakes, and an extensive trail system. Great spot for bird-watching.
Website: www.state.ma.us/mdc/breakhrt.htm
Location: Forest St., Saugus
Major Routes/Cross Streets: Rt. 1/Lynn Fells Parkway
Parking: free

Phone: 781-233-0834
Hours: Dawn to dusk
Cost: free
Discounts: n/a
Credit cards accepted: n/a
FREE admission hours: all
Food available at site: NO
Ages: 0-14
Available for Birthday parties? Yes but permit may be required-call
Changing station: no
Notes: __picnic area and tot lot, ranger conducted programs on plant & animal life, restrooms not presently available___

Lynn Woods Reservation
Over 2200 acres with 30 miles of trails for hiking and nature walks. Includes 'Dungeon Rock', an underground tunnel with a history of pirates and treasure.
Website: www.lynndpw.com/woods/lynnwood.htm
Location: 106 Pennybrook Road, Lynn

Major Routes/Cross Streets:
Walnut Street near Gannon golf
course
Parking: free parking lot
Phone: 781-598-4000 ext.6792
Hours: dawn to dusk
Cost: free
Discounts: n/a
Credit cards accepted: n/a
FREE admission hours: all
Food available at site: no
Ages: 0-14
Available for Birthday parties? call
Strollers allowed? yes
Changing station: no
Notes:_____

Endicott Park
The park is on the site of a former
dairy farm and has 165 acres to
explore. The park includes
woodlands, orchards, wetlands,
fields and buildings. There are also
ponds for fishing and wildlife
observation.
Website:
www.danversrec.com/endicott/inde
x.html

Location: Forrest St., Danvers
Major Routes/Cross Streets:
Rt.1/Rt.62
Parking: Fee $1 per car residents,
$3 per car non-residents
Phone: 978-777-0001 ext. 3094
Hours: 9am to dusk daily
Cost: parking fee – call for group
rates
Discounts: Danvers residents
Credit cards accepted: n/a
FREE admission hours: n/a
Food available at site: no
Ages: 0-14
Available for Birthday parties? call
Strollers allowed? yes
Changing station: no
Notes: Park includes historical sites
Glen Magna Mansion and Derby
Summers House (Tea House), there
is a fenced play space, barnyard
animals, and picnic ground.
Bathrooms in the carriage house

Harold Parker State Forest

Large park with 3000 acres and trails for walking/hiking. There is an annual Fishing Festival held in mid-August. There are also 11 ponds!

Website: www.state.ma.us/dem/parks/harp.htm

Location: 1951 Turnpike St., N. Andover

Major Routes/Cross Streets: Rt. 114

Parking: free parking in lot (also available parking in picnic area $5 and camping $10)

Phone: 978-686-3391

Hours: dawn to dusk

Cost: free

Discounts: n/a

Credit cards accepted: n/a

FREE admission hours: all

Food available at site: no

Ages: 0-14

Available for Birthday parties? yes

Strollers allowed? yes

Changing station: no

Notes: _Restrooms available Memorial Day to Labor Day at the pond_____

Great Brook Farm State Park

There are 20 miles of trails for walking or hiking in this 1000 acres park. This is an active dairy with lots of cows! Petting area too. There are barn tours on summer weekends. Also, canoeing is available on Meadow Pond.

Website: www.state.ma.us/dem/parks/gbfm.htm
Location: 984 Lowell Rd., Carlisle
Major Routes/Cross Streets: Rt.225
Parking: parking lot $2 fee
Phone: 978-369-6312
Hours: dawn to dusk
Cost: $2 parking fee
Discounts: n/a
Credit cards accepted: n/a
FREE admission hours: all
Food available at site: YES (ice-cream stand with drinks and food in summer)
Ages: 0-14

Available for Birthday parties? yes
Strollers allowed? yes
Changing station: no
Notes: _portable potty only. Can book private barn tours mid-week .

Area Fairs

The Marshfield Fair
When: Generally August
Where: Rt.3A Marshfield
Phone: 781-834-6629
Website: www.marshfieldfair.org

The Brockton Fair
When: Generally July
Where: Rt.123 Brockton
Phone: 508-586-8000
Website: www.brocktonfair.com

The Topsfield Fair
When: Generally October
Where: Rt.1 Topsfield
Phone: 978-887-5000
Website: www.topsfieldfair.org

Purgatory Chasm State Park

This park features a natural echo chamber in a 70-foot gorge. The gorge is almost a quarter mile long and was formed 14000 years ago. There are 5 trails to choose from with the longest one running about a mile. The kids will love climbing the boulders and checking out the caves. Park rangers also lead nature programs like THE AMIMAL DETECTIVE. NOTE: the hike involves "boulder scrambling" which can quickly tire smaller children - bring the backpack for little ones.

Website:www.state.ma.us/dem/parks/purg.htm

Location: Rte 146 Purgatory Road, Sutton

Major Routes/Cross Streets: Rt. 146

Parking: Free parking in lot

Phone: 508-234-3733 or the ranger's office at 508-234-9610

Hours: Dawn to Dusk
Cost: free
Discounts: N/A
Credit cards accepted: N/A
FREE admission hours: all
Food available at site: NO
Ages:0-14
Available for Birthday parties? call
Strollers allowed? N/A
Changing station: no
Notes: restrooms available

Broadmore Wildlife Sanctuary

Explore 9 miles of walking trails on this 624 acre sanctuary. A long bridge over Indian Brook provides a great spot for watching wildlife which may include beavers, otters and wood ducks.
Website: www.massaudubon.org
Location: 280 Elliot Street, Natick
Major Routes/Cross Streets: Rt. 16/Rt.27
Parking: parking lot
Phone: 508-655-2296
Hours: Nature Center open T-F 9-5, S,S & M holidays 10-5.
Trails are open dawn to dusk

Cost: A$4, S$3, C$3 (3-12)
Discounts: members
Credit cards accepted: MC, V
FREE admission hours: n/a
Food available at site: no
Ages: 0-14
Available for Birthday parties? no
Strollers allowed? yes
Changing station: no
Notes: <u>Restrooms are in the nature center</u>

Cochituate State Park
Three large lakes are included in this park. Enjoy nature walks, picnics and water fun. Kayak and canoe rentals available.
Website: <u>www.state.ma.us/dem/ parks/coch.html</u>
Location: Rt. 30, Natick
Major Routes/Cross Streets: Rt. 30
Parking: parking lot
Phone: 508-653-9641
Hours: dawn to dusk generally
Cost: $5 per car
Discounts: n/a
Credit cards accepted: n/a

FREE admission hours: n/a
Food available at site: ice cream truck
Ages: 0-14
Available for Birthday parties? no
Strollers allowed? yes
Changing station: yes
Notes: Accessible restrooms_____

Hopkinton State Park

Park includes 1450 acres for hiking, fishing, canoeing, mountain biking and picnicking. There is also a small beach and non-motorized boating is allowed
Website: www.state.ma.us/dem/parks/hpsp.htm
Location: Rt. 85. Hopkinton
Major Routes/Cross Streets: Rt.85/Rt.135
Parking: parking lot
Phone: 508-435-4303
Hours: dawn to dusk
Cost: $5 parking fee in summer
Discounts: n/a
Credit cards accepted: no
FREE admission hours: all

Food available at site: no
Ages: 0-14
Available for Birthday parties? yes
Strollers allowed? yes
Changing station: no
Notes: _restrooms available. Grills available by reservation in summer_____

Whitehall State Park
Whitehall Reservoir offers hiking, boating and fishing.
Website: www.state.ma.us/dem/parks/whit.htm
Location: Rt. 135, Hopkinton
Major Routes/Cross Streets: Rt.495/West Main St./Rt.135
Parking: free parking in lot
Phone: 508-435-4303
Hours: dawn to dusk generally
Cost: free
Discounts: n/a
Credit cards accepted: n/a
FREE admission hours: all
Food available at site: no
Ages: 0-14

Available for Birthday parties?
n/a
Strollers allowed? yes
Changing station: no
Notes: _____no restrooms_____

Miles Standish State Forest

Wonderful forest with 16 ponds. Enjoy hiking, nature walks, fishing and canoeing. Park offers programs in summer such as cranberry bog exploration and fire tower tours.

Website: www.state.ma.us/dem/parks/mssf.htm

Location: Cranberry Road South, Carver

Major Routes/Cross Streets: Rt.3/Rt.58

Parking: parking lot

Phone: 508-866-2526

Hours: dawn to dusk

Cost: free

Discounts: n/a

FREE admission hours: all

Ages: 0-14

Available for Birthday parties? n/a

Strollers allowed? yes

Changing station? no

Notes: restrooms available

MDC Blue Hills Reservation & Trailside Museum

Explore 150 miles of trails on the reservation. Museum exhibits feature live deer, otters, foxes and bobcats.

Website: www.massaudubon.org/nature_connection/sanctuaries/blue_hills/index.html

Or

www.state.ma.us/mdc/blue.htm

Location: 1904 Canton Ave., Milton

Major Routes/Cross Streets: Rt. 138

Phone: 617-333-0690

Parking: free parking in lot

Hours: Nature Center W-Su 10-5. Trails open dawn to dusk daily

Cost: A$3, S$2, C$1.50 (3-12)

Discounts: members

Credit cards accepted: MC, V

FREE admission hours: none

Food available at site: no

Ages: 0-14

Available for Birthday parties? yes

Strollers allowed: yes

Changing Station: no

Notes: _picnic area, restrooms available_____

CLASSES

Classes are a great way to explore new things, nurture a talent, meet new friends and have fun. There are many different types of classes offered in suburban Boston. This book lists some of the topics of classes commonly offered by the organizations. There may be additional classes in other subject areas as well.

Category Index

Please Note: This list will not include every class available on the subject. The information provided is current to the best of our knowledge at the time of publication. If you do find an error, please let us know. A listing in this book is not an endorsement or recommendation of Kiwi Publishing. All ages are for reference only. Parents should determine appropriateness of the activity. Activities and prices are subject to change at any time.

Art

Lexington Arts and Crafts Society

Classes offered: Teen pottery, oil and acrylic painting.
Location: 130 Waltham Street, Lexington
Major Routes/Cross Streets: Rt.128/Rt.225 (Massachusetts Avenue)
Phone: 781-862-5613
Parking: Free parking
Ages: 13+
Website: N/A
Available for parties: NO
Discounts: N/A
Notes:_____

Arts for Everyone

Classes offered: Drawing, painting, clay, and oil painting.
Location:18 Perry Street, North Andover

Major Routes/Cross Streets: off 495
Phone: 978-683-2999
Parking: street parking
Ages: 6+
Website: N/A
Available for parties: NO
Discounts: N/A
Notes: ___in home studio_____

Pentucket Arts Center Inc.

Classes offered: Children's theater, drawing, painting, cartooning, bookmaking, creative development for pre-schoolers, and costume design.
Location: 61 Wingate Street, Haverhill
Major Routes/Cross Streets: Rt.495/Rt.97/Rt.125
Phone: 978-374-2508
Parking: parking on street and in lot
Ages: 3-14
Website: N/A
Available for parties: N/A
Discounts: sibling discounts
Notes:_____

Western Suburbs

Danforth Museum School
Classes offered: drawing, painting, cartooning, multimedia, pottery, sculpture, jewelry, and photography.
Location: 123 Union Avenue, Framingham
Major Route/Cross Streets: Rt. 126
Phone: 508-620-0050
Parking: Free parking in lot
Ages: 4-14
Website: www.danforthmuseum.org
Available for parties: YES
Discounts: no
Notes: special 3 day school vacations workshops available

Franklin School for Performing Arts
Classes offered: music, voice, dance and drama. Classes are generally after school and there are many performance opportunities.
Location: 38 Main Street, Franklin

Major Route/Cross Streets: Rt. 140
Phone: 508-528-8668
Parking: street parking
Ages: 5-14
Website: www.FSPAonline.com
Available for parties: No
Discounts: N/A
Notes: _____

Arts Center at Southboro
Classes offered: "Tunes for Tots", Art Exploration, Pottery, Basic Beaded Jewelry
Location: 21 Highland Street, Southboro
Major Route/Cross Street: Rt.9/Cordaville Road
Phone: 508-481-9351
Parking: parking area, parties: n/a, discounts: call
Ages: 2-12
Website: N/A
Available for parties:
Discounts:
Notes:_____

Cultural Arts Alliance
Classes offered: art exploration, "Musikgarten", drawing, young writers workshop and private music lessons (piano, guitar, etc.)
Location: 98 Hayden Rowe Street, Hopkinton
Major Routes/Cross Streets: Rt. 85
Phone: 508-435-9222
Parking: Free parking in lot
Ages: 0-10
Website: www.hcaa.fiam.net
Available for parties: N/A
Discounts: sibling discounts
Notes:_____

Art Lessons of the Rotary
Classes offered: drawing classes
Location: 3 South Street, Westboro
Major Routes/Cross Streets: Rt.135/Rt.30
Phone: 508-898-3279
Parking: parking area
Ages: 6-14
Website: N/A
Available for parties: N/A
Discounts: n/a

Notes: Classes focus on drawing cartoon characters, robots, etc.

Angela's School of Performing Arts
Classes offered: art projects
Location: 280 Ridge Street, Millis
Major Routes/Cross Streets: Rt.27/Exchange Street
Phone: 508-376-4099
Parking: parking area
Ages: 3-14
Website: no
Available for parties: n/a
Discounts: family discounts
Notes:_____

Potter's School and Shop
Classes offered: Children's classes include pottery instruction with use of potter's wheel. Classes meet Saturday mornings.
Location: 31 Thorpe Road, Needham Heights
Major Route/Cross Streets: Rt.135/Webster Street
Phone: 781-449-7687
Parking: street parking

Ages: school age
Website: www.artfulgift.com/arts/
potters.htm
Available for parties: yes
Discounts: N/A
Notes:_____

New Arts Center in Newton
Classes offered: Drama, ceramics,
photography, cartooning, and
dance. Classes are after school and
on Saturdays.
Location: 61 Washington Park,
Newton
Major Route/Cross Streets:
Rt.16/Walnut Street
Phone: 617-964-3424
Parking: street parking
Ages: 2-14
Website: www.newtonartcenter.org
Available for parties: YES
Discounts: N/A
Notes:_____

Superstarts
Classes offered: Creative art classes
Location: 46 Brentwood Circle, Needham
Major Route/Cross Streets:
Phone: 781-444-5496
Parking: street parking, major routes/cross streets: 135
Ages: 18 months to 7 years
Website: no
Available for parties: n/a
Discounts: n/a
Notes:_____

The Kids Place
Classes offered: Drop in art studio. Classes include optiart and candle projects. Kids can decorate projects and take them home the same day. Children over 5 may be dropped off for up to 1 hour.
Location: 388 Watertown Street, Newton
Major Route/Cross Streets: Rt.16
Phone: 617-527-0500

Parking: street parking
Ages: 5-8
Website: www.kidplaceforfun.com
Available for parties: YES
Discounts: N/A
Notes:_____

Telamon Community Center
Classes offered: expressive art-drawing, writing and more
Location: 14 School St., Medway
Major Routes/Cross Streets:
Rt.109/Holliston Street
Phone: 508-533-2400
Parking: parking lot
Ages: 6-13
Website: www.telamonctr.com
Available for parties: no
Discounts: members
Notes:_____

Coupons for family stuff:

The following websites offer
coupons for useful family items
such as food, toys and clothes:
www.smartsource.com
www.shoppersesource.com
www.momsview.com
www.coolsavings.com
www.freebieville.com

Southern Suburbs

Artists' Way
Classes offered: pottery, watercolors
Location: 263 North Main Street, Mansfield
Major Route/Cross Streets: Rt.140/Rt.206
Phone: 508-339-0855
Parking: street parking
Ages: 4+
Website: no
Available for parties: n/a
Discounts: no
Notes: _ summer "camps" too_____

Fuller Museum of Art
Classes offered: sculpture, water colors, drawing, cartooning, clay tiles, photography and fashion illustration. All classes are offered through the museum school.
Location: 455 Oak Street, Brockton
Major Route/Cross Streets: Rt.24/Rt/27

Phone: 508-588-6000
Parking: parking lot
Ages: 0-4 for Kids Korner, 5+ for classes
Website: www.fullermuseum.org
Available for parties: n/a
Discounts: n/a
Notes:_Kids Korner offers drop in morning playtime with songs and stories for children 0-4_____

Potter's Place
Classes offered: pottery
Location:125 West Street, Walpole
Major Routes/Cross Streets: Rt. 27
Phone: 508-668-0363
Parking: parking lot
Ages: 1st grade +
Website: no
Available for parties: yes
Discounts: n/a
Notes: _summer camps too_____

Free Art/Craft Classes for Kids

A.C. Moore   www.acmoore.com
Classes held in:

Brockton	508-584-9933
Woburn	781-938-8391
Danvers	978-750-0420
Framingham	508-620-7560
Bellingham	508-966-3335
Dartmouth	508-992-4441

Michael's   www.michaels.com
Classes held in:

Natick	508-651-2225
Attleboro	508-643-2565
Shrewsbury	508-755-2900
Avon	508-580-8881
Braintree	781-848-6565
Burlington	781-229-7592
Hanover	781-829-6571

Dance

Children's Arts Corner
Classes offered: pre-ballet, ballet, creative dance, jazz
Location: 1403 Massachusetts Ave., Lexington
Major Routes/Cross Streets: Rt.95/Rt.128/Rt.225/Rt.4
Phone: 781-862-3117
Parking: free parking
Ages: 3-14
Website: www.artscorner.com
Available for parties: yes
Discounts: n/a
Notes: __summer camp too_____

The Dance Inn (Munrow Center for Arts)
Classes offered: Introduction to dance, jazz, tap, hip-hop, technique and more.
Location: 1403 Massachusetts Ave., Fl 2 Lexington
Major Routes/Cross Streets: Rt.4/Rt.225/Bedford St
Phone: 781-861-9349
Parking: parking area
Ages: 3-14
Website: www.thedanceinn.com
Available for parties: n/a
Discounts: family discounts
Notes: Annual recital. Summer theater and Dance camps.____

School of Ballet Arts
Classes offered: ballet
Location: 2600 Massachusetts Ave., Lexington
Major Routes/Cross Streets: Rt.4/Rt.225
Phone: 781-862-2683

Parking: parking area
Ages: 4.5 -14
Website: no
Available for parties: no
Discounts: n/a
Notes:_____

Miss Tina's II
Classes offered: creative movement, ballet, tap, jazz
Location: 77 Maple St., Danvers
Major Routes/Cross Streets: Rt.62
Phone: 978-777-0337
Parking: parking area
Ages: 2-14
Website: n/a
Available for parties: n/a
Discounts: family and volume discounts
Notes:_____

Miss Tina's Dance Studio
Classes offered: creative movement, ballet, tap, jazz
Location: 28 Burnham St., Gloucester
Major Routes/Cross Streets: Rt.128/Prospect Street

Phone: 978-283-8758
Parking: parking area
Ages: 2-14
Website: n/a
Available for parties: n/a
Discounts: family and volume discounts
Notes:_____

Dawn's Studio of Dance
Classes offered: ballet, tap, acrobatics , jazz
Location: 271 Main St., Gloucester
Major Routes/Cross Streets: Rt.128/Main Street/School Street
Phone: 978-283-9251
Parking: behind senior home care
Ages: 2-14
Website: www.dawnsstudio.com
Available for parties: n/a
Discounts: multiple class discounts
Notes:_____

Dance Explosions
Classes offered: ballet, acrobatics and more
Location: 7 River St., Middleton
Major Routes/Cross Streets: Rt.128/Rt.114
Phone: 978-762-8300
Parking: parking area
Ages: 2.5-14
Website: n/a
Available for parties: call
Discounts: some-call
Notes: _____

Dance with Dena
Classes offered: jazz, cheer/dance, tap, hip-hop, ballet
Location: 59 Main St., Peabody
Major Routes/Cross Streets: Rt.128/Rt.114/Central Street
Phone: 978-531-7618
Parking: parking area
Ages: 3-14
Website: no
Available for parties: no

Discounts: n/a
Notes: __summer dance workshops available_____

Deane School of Dance
Classes offered: ballet, tap, jazz, lyrical jazz
Location: 84 Hawthorne St., Salem
Major Routes/Cross Streets: Rt.1A
Phone: 978-745-0465
Parking: yes
Ages: 2.5-14
Website: n/a
Available for parties: no
Discounts: no
Notes:_____

Marblehead School of Ballet
Classes offered: ballet, modern, creative movement, pre-ballet
Location: 115 Pleasant St., Marblehead
Major Routes/Cross Streets: Rt.114
Phone: 781-631-6262
Parking: parking area
Ages: generally 4+

Website:
www.havetodance.com/marblehead.htm
Available for parties: no
Discounts: n/a
Notes: __studio is upstairs next to theater_____

Dance New England
Classes offered: kinderbasics, ballet, tap, jazz, hip-hop, toddler gym, street funk, Irish Step, modern
Location: 51 Middlesex Street, North Chelmsford
Major Routes/Cross Streets: Rt.3A
Phone: 978-535-5147
Parking: parking area
Ages: 2-14
Website:
www.dancenewengland.com
Available for parties: n/a
Discounts: family discounts
Notes: __summer intensives available__

Joyce Dance Studio
Classes offered: ballet, tap
Location: 216 Main St., Amesbury
Major Routes/Cross Streets:
Rt.495
Phone: 978-388-1764
Parking: parking area
Ages: 3+
Website: no
Available for parties: no
Discounts: n/a
Notes:_____

Yang's Andover – Martial Arts and Fitness
Classes offered: hip-hop jazz,
ballet, tap, combo ballet/tap
Location: 65 Flagship Drive, North
Andover
Major Routes/Cross Streets:
Rt.114/Rt.125
Phone: 978-725-3600
Parking: parking lot
Ages: 3.5-14
Website: www.dance-moves.com
Available for parties: n/a
Discounts: n/a
Notes:_____

Studio for Dance
Classes offered: pre-ballet, ballet, tap, jazz, hip-hop, lyrical, pointe and more
Location: 6 Washington St., North Reading
Major Routes/Cross Streets: Rt.128 exit 40
Phone: 978-664-3780
Parking: parking lot
Ages: 3 -14
Website: no
Available for parties: no
Discounts: n/a
Notes: _studio is located in small strip-mall_____

Center Stage Dance Academy
Classes offered: ballet, tap, jazz and more
Location: 199 Washington St., Haverhill
Major Routes/Cross Streets: Rt.495/ Washington Street
Phone: 978-372-8554
Parking: parking area
Ages: 3-14

Website: no
Available for parties: starting in September
Discounts: n/a
Notes:_____

Karla Pattavina's Dance Academy
Classes offered: ballet, tap, baton, jazz
Location: 371 River St., Haverhill
Major Routes/Cross Streets: Rt.495/River Street
Phone: 978-372-9070
Parking: parking lot
Ages: 3+
Website: www.dance-academy.com
Available for parties: no
Discounts: n/a
Notes:_____

Sally Gould Dance Center
Classes offered: mommy & me dance, ballet, tap, jazz, hip-hop
Location: 210 Boston Road, Chelmsford
Major Routes/Cross Streets: Rt.4
Phone: 978-256-3183
Parking: parking area

Ages: generally 3+
Website: no
Available for parties: no
Discounts: some - call
Notes:_____

North Shore Dance Academy
Classes offered: tap, ballet, jazz, lyrical, acrobatics
Location: 282 Cabot Street #A, Beverly
Major Routes/Cross Streets: Rt.97/Rt.1A
Phone: 978-921-0249
Parking: parking area
Ages: 3-14
Website: no
Available for parties: no
Discounts: family discounts
Notes: summer programs available_____

Hamilton-Wenham School of Dance
Classes offered: creative movement, ballet, jazz, modern
Location: 15 Walnut Road, Hamilton

Major Routes/Cross Streets: At128/Rt.1A
Phone: 978-468-2393
Parking: parking area
Ages: 4-14
Website: no
Available for parties: no
Discounts: no
Notes:_____

Tricia's Tots Preschool Dance
Classes offered: basic movement, rhythm, ballet
Location: 11 Independence Avenue, Tewksbury
Major Routes/Cross Streets: Rt.38/Shawsheen Street
Phone: 978-851-6160
Parking: street parking
Ages: 2-6
Website: no
Available for parties: no
Discounts: n/a
Notes: in-home studio_____

Dancing Connection Inc.
Classes offered: hip-hop, swing and more
Location: 113 Dodge St., Beverly
Major Routes/Cross Streets: Rt.128/Rt.1A/ Rt.197
Phone: 978-922-7755
Parking: free parking in lot
Ages: 3-14
Website: www.dancingconnections.com
Available for parties: no
Discounts: family and multiple class discounts
Notes:_____

Burlington Dancer's Workshop
Classes offered: ballet, tap, jazz
Location: 35 Winn St., Burlington
Major Routes/Cross Streets: Rt.128/Rt.95/Winn Street
Phone: 781-272-2762
Parking: parking lot
Ages: 3-14
Website: no
Available for parties: no
Discounts: n/a
Notes:_____

Ballet Arts Center-Winchester
Classes offered: creative movement, boys funk, pre-ballet, ballet, jazz, tap, pointe
Location: 50 Cross St., Winchester
Major Routes/Cross Streets: Rt.38
Phone: 781-729-8556
Parking: off-street parking
Ages: 3-14
Website: www.bacw.com
Available for parties: no
Discounts: n/a
Notes: many performance opportunities

Belmont School of Dance
Classes offered: pre-school, ballet, tap, jazz
Location: 697 Belmont St., Belmont
Major Routes/Cross Streets: Rt.128/Rt/2
Phone: 617-484-5618
Parking: street parking
Ages: 3-14
Website: no

Available for parties: no
Discounts: n/a
Notes:*closes for summer_____

Agnes Strecker Dance Studio
Classes offered: dance with mommy, play dance, jazz, hip-hop, tumbling, cheer dance, hula dance, musical theater
Location: 150 Main St., Reading
Major Routes/Cross Streets: Rt.28
Phone: 781-942-8709
Parking: parking area
Ages: 1-14
Website: no
Available for parties: no
Discounts: multiple class discounts
Notes: ___private and semi-private classes available_____

Let's Dance Inc.
Classes offered: ballet, lyrical, acrobatics
Location: 79 Central St. Stoneham
Major Routes/Cross Streets: Rt.93/Montvale Avenue
Phone: 781-438-3166
Parking: parking area

Ages: 2-14
Website: no
Available for parties: yes
Discounts: n/a
Notes:_ summer camp too_____

Ellen's School of Dance
Classes offered: ballet, tap, jazz, preschool, gymnastics, Riverdance, lyrical, street funk
Location: 767 Boston Road, Billerica
Major Routes/Cross Streets: Rt.3A
Phone: 978-667-3441
Parking: parking area
Ages: 3-14
Website: no
Available for parties: no
Discounts: no
Notes:_____

Ellen's School of Dance
Classes offered: ballet, tap, jazz, preschool, gymnastics, Riverdance, lyrical, street funk
Location: 120 Cambridge St., Burlington
Major Routes/Cross Streets: Rt.3A

Phone: 781-229-9099
Parking: parking area
Ages: 3-14
Website: no
Available for parties: no
Discounts: no
Notes:_____

Ellen's School of Dance
Classes offered: ballet, tap, jazz, preschool, gymnastics, Riverdance, lyrical, street funk
Location: 18 Pond View Place, Tyngsboro
Major Routes/Cross Streets: Rt.3A
Phone: 978-649-3302
Parking: parking area
Ages: 3-14
Website: no
Available for parties: no
Discounts: no
Notes:_____

One Stop Fun Inc.
Classes offered: dance, cheerleading
Location: 49 Power Road, Westford
Major Routes/Cross Streets: Rt.495/Rt.2A
Phone: 978-692-9907
Parking: parking lot
Ages: 3-14
Website: www.onestopfun.com
Available for parties: yes
Discounts: sibling discounts
Notes: _vacation camps and team camps too_____

Ballet Workshop New England

Classes offered: creative movement, pre-ballet and graded ballet.
Location: 56 Hayden Rowe, Hopkinton
Major Routes/Cross Streets: Rt.85
Phone: 508-435-5600
Parking: street parking
Ages: Creative movement for 3 and 4 year olds. Pre-ballet for 5 year olds and graded ballet classes for all levels.
Website: www.massyouthballet.org
Available for parties: no
Discounts: n/a
Notes: programs for boys and girls-performing opportunities

Ballet Workshop New England

Classes offered: creative movement, pre-ballet and graded ballet.
(programs for boys and girls-performing opportunities)
Location: 411 Waverly Oaks Road, Waltham
Major Routes/Cross Streets: Rt.60

Phone: 781-894-8484
Parking: parking area
Ages: Creative movement for 3 and 4 year olds. Pre-ballet for 5 year olds and graded ballet classes for all levels.
Website: www.massyouthballet.org
Available for parties: no
Discounts: n/a
Notes:_____

Peggy McGlone Dance Studio
Classes offered: ballet, tumbling and more
Location: 621 Main St., Waltham
Major Routes/Cross Streets: Rt.128
Phone: 781-893-6139
Parking: parking area-municipal lot across street
Ages: 18 months-14
Website: no
Available for parties: no
Discounts: n/a

Notes:_____

Franklin School for Performing Arts
Classes offered: ballet, pointe, jazz, tap, modern, hip-hop, children's dance, boys dance
Location: 38 Main Street, Franklin
Major Route/Cross Streets: Rt. 140
Phone: 508-528-8668
Parking: street parking
Ages: 5-14
Website: www.FSPAonline.com
Available for parties: No
Discounts: N/A
Notes: _____

Charlotte Klein Dance Centers
Classes offered: Terrific Twos, Creative Movement, Kinderdance, Danceworks, ballet, pointe, modern and tap/jazz.
Location: 164 Milk Street, Westboro (In Westmeadow Plaza)
Major Routes/Cross Streets: Rt. 135
Phone: 508-366-8961

Parking: free parking in lot
Ages: 2-14
Website: www.ckdance.com
Available for parties: n/a
Discounts: prompt payment
discount
Notes:_____

Laurene Aldorisio Academy of Dance Expression

Classes offered: ballet, pointe,
kinderdance, pre-ballet, jazz,
modern, tap
Location: 45 E Main Street,
Westboro
Major Routes/Cross Streets: Rt.30
Phone: 508-836-3608
Parking: parking lot
Ages: 3-14
Website:
www.laurenedanceexpressions.com
Available for parties: no
Discounts: n/a
Notes:_____

Patricia Brosnihan Dance Center
Classes offered: pre-school dance, ballet, tap, jazz
Location: 77 W. Main Street, Hopkinton
Major Routes/Cross Streets: Rt.495
Phone: 508-435-5312
Parking: parking lot
Ages: 2.5-14
Website: no
Available for parties: no
Discounts: family discounts
Notes: __mini ballet and jazz summer camps__

Backstage Dance Center
Classes offered: creative dance, movement foundations, boys on the move, ballet/tap, ballet/jazz, jazz, hip-hop, musical theater, pointe
Location: 300 Elliot St, Ashland
Phone: 508-881-8226
Major Routes/Cross Streets: Rt.135/Rt.126
Parking: parking lot
Ages: 1-14
Website: no

Available for parties: yes
Discounts: n/a
Notes: _opportunities to audition for
performances too!_____

Dancing Arts Center
Classes offered: ballet, modern,
creative movement, pre-ballet, pre-
modern, jazz
Location: 781 Washington St,
Holliston
Phone: 508-429-7577
Major Routes/Cross Streets:
Rt.16/Rt.126
Parking: street parking or parking
lot in back
Ages: 3-14
Website:
www.dancingartscenter.com
Available for parties: yes
Discounts: family discounts
Notes:_____

Diane's School of Dance
Classes offered: ballet, tap, jazz,
lyrical, tumbling
Location: 27 Oak Drive, Upton
Phone: 508-529-6409

Major Routes/Cross Streets:
Rt.140/Mendon Street/South Street
Parking: parking area
Ages: 2.9 -14
Website: no
Available for parties: no
Discounts: n/a
Notes:_____

Performing Arts Center-Metrowest
Classes offered: jazz, creative
dance, hip-hop, ballet, swing, tap
Location: 140 Pearl Street,
Framingham
Major Routes/Cross Streets:
Rt.135/Rt.126
Phone: 508-875-5554
Parking: parking lot
Ages: 3-14
Website: N/A
Available for parties: No
Discounts: members
Notes:_____

Dancing Arts Center
Classes offered: ballet, modern,
creative movement

Location: 1 Pleasant St,
Framingham
Major Routes/Cross Streets: Rt.30
Phone: 508-875-0931
Parking: parking area
Ages: 3-14
Website:
www.dancingartscenter.com
Available for parties: yes
Discounts: family discounts
Notes:_____

<u>Millis School of Dance</u>
Classes offered: ballet, pointe, tap.
Jazz, lyrical, musical theater,
modern, kinder movement, tiny tots,
tumble tots and acro tots
Location: 30 Exchange Street, Millis
Major Routes/Cross Streets:
Rt.109/Rt.115
Phone: 508-376-8030
Parking: parking lot
Ages: 3-14
Website:
www.millisschoolofdance.com
Available for parties: no
Discounts: family discounts
Notes:_____

Rosemarie's Dance Studio/RDS Performing Arts

Classes offered: pre-school ballet, intro to ballet, classical ballet/pointe, tap, jazz
Location: 32 Dedham Street, Dover
Major Routes/Cross Streets: Rt.16/ Pleasant Street
Phone: 508-785-2027
Parking: parking area
Ages: 3-14
Website: no
Available for parties: no
Discounts: some
Notes:_____

Le Studio Danse

Classes offered: ballet, jazz, hip-hop, classical, music video
Location: 184 N Main Street, Mansfield
Major Routes/Cross Streets: Rt.140/Rt.106
Phone: 508-339-7666
Parking: parking lot
Ages: 4-14
Website: no

Available for parties: no
Discounts: some
Notes: _____

Angela's School of Performing Arts
Classes offered: ballet, tap, jazz, lyrical
Location: 280 Ridge Street, Millis
Major Routes/Cross Streets:
Rt.115/Orchard Street
Phone: 508-376-4099
Parking: parking area
Ages: 3-14
Website: no
Available for parties: no
Discounts: family discounts
Notes:_____

Sue's Dance Studio
Classes offered: ballet, tap, jazz, hip-hop
Location: 31 Main Street, Marlboro
Major Routes/Cross Streets:
Rt.495/Rt.20
Phone: 508-485-3518
Parking: parking area
Ages: 3-14

Website: no
Available for parties: no
Discounts: family discounts
Notes:_____

Dawn's School of Dance
Classes offered: ballet, jazz, acrobatics
Location: 369 W. Main Street, Northboro
Major Routes/Cross Streets: Rt.20/Rt.9/Rt.495/Rt.290
Phone: 508-393-9753
Parking: parking area
Ages: 3-14
Website: no
Available for parties: no
Discounts: some
Notes: __closed summers_____

Dance it Up! Dance Center
Classes offered: Ballet, modern, tap, jazz, "Just for boys", "Team Dance it up", "Dance n play", and Irish Step dancing.
Location: 36 N. Main Street Rte. 140, North Grafton, MA

Major Routes/Cross Streets:
Rt.140
Phone: 508-839-1648
Parking: parking area
Ages: 2.5-14
Website: no
Available for parties: no
Discounts: some
Notes:_____

<u>Needham Dance Theater</u>
Classes offered: ballet, tap, jazz
Location: 22 Chestnut St, Needham
Major Routes/Cross Streets:
Rt.128
Phone: 781-449-5585
Parking: parking area
Ages: 3-14
Website: no
Available for parties: yes
Discounts: family discounts
Notes:_____

Nancy Kelley Dance Studio
Classes offered: ballet, jazz, hip-hop, acrobatic, baton
Location: 7 Pond Street, Natick
Major Routes/Cross Streets: Rt.9/Rt.27
Phone: 508-655-0332
Parking: parking area
Ages: 2.5 -14
Website: no
Available for parties: no
Discounts: no
Notes:_____

Paulette's Ballet Studio
Classes offered: ballet, pre-ballet, jazz, hip-hop, pointe, lyrical, modern, tap, musical theater, choreography, swing and Irish Step.
Location: 190 Oak Street, Newton
Major Routes/Cross Streets: Rt.9/Chestnut Street
Phone: 617-527-9565
Parking: parking area
Ages: 8-14
Website: www.pauletteballetstudio.com

Available for parties: only for students
Discounts: call
Notes: _summer intensive_____

Paulette's Ballet Studio
Classes offered: ballet, pre-ballet, jazz, hip-hop, pointe, lyrical, modern, tap, musical theater, choreography, swing and Irish Step.
Location: 93 West Street, Medfield
Major Routes/Cross Streets: Rt.109/Rt.27
Phone: 508-359-5192
Parking: parking area
Ages: 8-14
Website: www.pauletteballetstudio.com
Available for parties: only for students
Discounts: call
Notes: __summer intensive_____

All That Jazz
Classes offered: ballet, tap, and jazz.
Location: 230 California St., Newton
Major Routes/Cross Streets: Rt.90
Phone: 617-641-0784
Parking: street parking
Ages: 2 - 14
Website: no
Available for parties: YES
Discounts: multiple sibling discount
Notes: no registration fee

Joanne Langione Dance Center
Classes offered: tap, jazz, lyrical and more
Location: 35 Border St., Newton
Major Routes/Cross Streets: Rt.16/Elm Street
Phone: 617-969-8724
Parking: limited parking in lot. Municipal lot available a short distance away.
Ages: 18 months -14
Website: www.jldancecenter.com
Available for parties: yes
Discounts: n/a

Notes:_____

Stage Door Dance Theater
Classes offered: ballet, tap jazz
Location: 796 Boston Post Road
East, Marlboro
Major Routes/Cross Streets: Rt.20
Phone: 508-786-0350
Parking: parking lot
Ages: 3-14
Website: www.stagedoordance.com
Available for parties: no
Discounts: multiple class discounts
Notes:_____

Walpole Dance Center
Classes offered: ballet, tap, jazz
Location: 948 Main Street, Walpole
Major Routes/Cross Streets:
Rt.1/Rt.27
Phone: 508-668-8370
Parking: street parking
Ages: 3-14
Website: no
Available for parties: no
Discounts: family discounts
Notes:_____

Commonwealth Dance Academy
Classes offered: preschool ballet,
tap, jazz, pointe
Location: 306 Elm Street, Walpole
Phone: 508-668-4764
Major Routes/Cross Streets: Rt.27
Parking: parking area
Ages: 3-14
Website:
www.commonwealthdance.com
Available for parties: yes,
weekends only
Discounts: some

Notes:_____

Medfield Dance Academy
Classes offered: preschool, tots, ballet, hip-hop, tap, jazz, pre-pointe, pointe, baton
Location: 14 N Meadows Rd, Medfield
Major Routes/Cross Streets: Rt.27/Rt.109
Phone: 508-359-9665
Parking: parking area
Ages: 2-14
Website: www.medfielddance.com
Available for parties: yes
Discounts: early payment discount
Notes:_____

O'Brien's School of Dance
Classes offered: tap, jazz, hip-hop, ballet, Irish Step
Location: 16 Railroad Avenue, Foxboro
Major Routes/Cross Streets: Rt. 495
Phone: 508-543-3949
Parking: parking area
Ages: 3-14

Website: no
Available for parties: no
Discounts: some
Notes:_____

Studio One Academy of Dance
Classes offered: preschool program, tap, ballet, jazz, gymnastics
Location: 148 Howard St., Brockton
Major Routes/Cross Streets:
Rt.24/ Harrison Boulevard
Phone: 508-588-0147
Parking: parking area
Ages: 3-14
Website: no
Available for parties: no
Discounts: no
Notes:_____

Matta Dance Academy
Classes offered: ballet, tap, jazz and more
Location: 311 North Warren Ave., Brockton
Major Routes/Cross Streets: Rt. 24/Rt.28
Phone: 508-586-4687
Parking: parking area

Ages: 3.5 -14
Website: no
Available for parties: yes
Discounts: family discounts
Notes:_____

Joan's Olympic Gym & Fitness
Classes offered: ballet, tap, jazz, gymnastics and more
Location: 197 Quincy Ave., Braintree
Major Routes/Cross Streets: Rt.53
Phone: 781-843-9624
Parking: parking area
Ages: 2-14
Website: no
Available for parties: no
Discounts: family discounts
Notes:_____

Sherry Gold Dance Studios
Classes offered: ballet, tap, jazz, modern, acrobatics, creative movement, Kindercombo
Location: 1154 North Montello St., Brockton
Major Routes/Cross Streets: Rt.24/Harrison Boulevard

Phone: 508-584-5499
Parking: parking area
Ages: 3-14
Website: www.renniegold.com
Available for parties: no
Discounts: family discounts
Notes:_____

Kalia Karr Studio of Dance
Classes offered: ballet, tap, jazz,
lyrical, pointe
Location: 105 Charles Eldridge
Road, Lakeville
Major Routes/Cross Streets:
Rt.495/Rt.78/Rt.105
Phone: 508-947-1899
Parking: parking area
Ages: 3-14
Website: no
Available for parties: no
Discounts: some-call
Notes:_____

Susan Winter School of Dance
Classes offered: ballet, tap
Location: 1250 New State Highway,
Raynham

Major Routes/Cross Streets:
Rt.495
Phone: 508-822-2029
Parking: parking area
Ages: 3-14
Website: no
Available for parties: yes
Discounts: family discounts
Notes:_____

Fontaine Academy of Dance
Classes offered: ballet, tap, jazz, modern, pre-ballet, dance teams and more
Location: 27 Railroad Ave., Duxbury
Major Routes/Cross Streets: Rt.3
Phone: 781-934-7393
Parking: parking area
Ages: 3.5-14
Website: no
Available for parties: no
Discounts: family discounts
Notes:_____

Dance Carousel
Classes offered: tap, ballet, jazz
Location: 28 Driftway, Scituate
Major Routes/Cross Streets: Rt.34
Phone: 781-545-7881
Parking: Street parking
Ages: 2.5-14
Website: no
Available for parties: no
Discounts: family discounts
Notes: ___summer programs too___

Cathy-Jo Irvine Dance Studio
Classes offered: tap, jazz, ballet, hip-hop
Location: 209 Water St., Pembroke
Major Routes/Cross Streets: Rt.53/Rt.139
Phone: 781-829-0733
Parking: parking area
Ages: 3-14
Website: no
Available for parties: no
Discounts: family discounts
Notes: _summer camp too_____

Duval Dance Studio
Classes offered: tap, ballet, modern, hi-hop
Location: 122 Front St., Scituate
Major Routes/Cross Streets: Rt.3A/First Parish Road/Beaver Dam Road
Phone: 781-545-3100
Parking: parking area
Ages: 3-14
Website: no
Available for parties: yes
Discounts: yes
Notes:_____

Susan's Studio of Dance
Classes offered: tap, ballet, jazz
Location: 270 Main St., Hanson
Major Routes/Cross Streets: Rt.27/Rt.58
Phone: 781-293-2188
Parking: off street parking
Ages: 3-14
Website: no
Available for parties: no
Discounts: some-call
Notes:__ summer camp in July____

Dance Workshop of Hanover

Classes offered: creative movement/pre-ballet, ballet, tap, modern, hip-hop, jazz
Location: 333 Columbia Road, Hanover
Major Routes/Cross Streets: Rt.3/Rt.53/Rt.139
Phone: 781-829-0390
Parking: parking lot
Ages: 2.5-14
Website: http://d.w.h.tripod.com
Available for parties: no
Discounts: n/a
Notes:_____

A Dancer's World

Classes offered: creative movement, pre-school dance, kinderdance, tap, ballet, and more
Location: 430 Plymouth St., Halifax
Major Routes/Cross Streets: Rt.495
Phone: 781-294-7969
Parking: parking area
Ages: 2.5-14
Website: no
Available for parties: no

Discounts: family discounts
Notes:_____

Marie Austin School of Dance
Classes offered: tap, ballet, jazz, hip-hop, lyrical
Location: 120 Hartsuff St., Rockland
Major Routes/Cross Streets: Rt.3
Phone: 781-878-1383
Parking: parking area
Ages: 2-14
Website: no
Available for parties: no
Discounts: some-call
Notes: __summer camp and dance teams_____

Michelle's Studio of Dance
Classes offered: ballet, tap, jazz, gymnastics, cheerdance, dance technique
Location: 649 Oak St., East Bridgewater
Major Routes/Cross Streets: Rt.14
Phone: 508-690-1350
Parking: parking lot
Ages: 3-14

Website: no
Available for parties: yes
Discounts: family discounts
Notes:__summer camp too

Kerry Smith's Academy of Dance Arts
Classes offered: pre-ballet, creative movement, ballet, tap, jazz, boy's class (music video dance & tap), music video dance
Location: 486 Washington Street, Norwood
Major Routes/Cross Streets: Rt.95/Rt.1
Phone: 781-762-3434
Parking: street parking
Ages: 3-14
Website: www.kerrysmithada.com
Available for parties: no
Discounts: family discount registration fees
Notes:_____

Norwood School of Ballet
Classes offered: pre-ballet, creative movement, ballet (all levels)
Location: 60 Day Street, Norwood

Major Routes/Cross Streets:
Rt.95/Rt.1
Phone: 781-769-2507
Parking: street parking
Ages: 3-14
Website: no
Available for parties: no
Discounts: none
Notes:_____

Language

Northern Suburbs

Children's Arts Corner
Classes offered: French & Spanish
Location: 1403 Massachusetts Ave., Lexington
Major Routes/Cross Streets: Rt.2/Rt.4/Rt.225
Phone: 781-862-3117
Parking: parking area
Ages: 3-12
Website: www.artscorner.com
Available for parties: no
Discounts: n/a
Notes: summer camp too

French for Kids
Classes offered: French classes offered weekly after school with games and songs as well as other creative approaches.
Location: 755 Massachusetts Ave., Lexington
Major Routes/Cross Streets: Rt.2/Rt.4/Rt.225

Phone: 781-863-6240
Parking: street parking, very limited on-site parking
Ages: 4-12
Website: www.frenchforkids.org
Available for parties: no
Discounts: n/a
Notes: located in The Follen Church

The Language Workshop for Children

Classes offered: French and Spanish for "tots" and children after school.
Location: 21 Church Street, Winchester
Major Routes/Cross Streets: Rt.3/Rt.38
Phone: 800-609-5484
Parking: parking area
Ages: 6 months–8 years
Website: no
Available for parties: no
Discounts: family discounts
Notes:_____

Music Connection

Classes offered: French and Spanish classes

Location: 38 Enon St., #R, Beverly

Major Routes/Cross Streets: Rt.1A

Phone: 978-921-7997

Parking: parking area

Ages: 0-14-family class

Website: www.kidsworks.net

Available for parties: yes

Discounts: no

Notes:_____

Arte Y Juego

Classes offered: Art and play in Spanish.
Location: Chestnut Hill
Major Routes/Cross Streets: Rt.9
Phone: 617-325-3773
Parking: parking area
Ages: 18 months to 8 years
Website: n/a
Available for parties: n/a
Discounts: n/a
Notes:_____

The Language Workshop for Children

Classes offered: French and Spanish for "tots" and children after school.
Location: 11 Homer Street, Newton
Major Routes/Cross Streets: Center Street/Homer Street
Phone: 800-609-5484
Parking: parking area
Ages: 6 months–8 years
Website: no
Available for parties: no

Discounts: family discounts
Notes:_____

Berlitz Language Center
Classes offered: French, German, Spanish, Italian, English and more
Location: 40 Washington St. #237, Wellesley
Major Routes/Cross Streets: Rt.16
Phone: 781-237-2220
Parking: parking lot
Ages: 4-14
Website: www.berlitz.com
Available for parties: no
Discounts: call
Notes: ___individual and group instruction available_____

Adventures in Languages
Classes offered: Spanish, French, Italian, Portuguese, Russian
Location: 10 Main St., Northboro
Major Routes/Cross Streets: Rt.20
Phone: 508-353-2730
Parking: parking lot
Ages: 2-14
Website: n/a
Available for parties: n/a

Discounts: n/a
Notes: Home-school programs available. Summer programs too!

Story Hours
Children's Story hours are held at many libraries and local Barns and Noble and Borders booksellers.

Barns and Noble locations:
Bellingham   508-966-7600
Framingham   508-628-5567
Walpole   508-668-1303
Chestnut Hill   617-965-7621
Burlington   781-273-3871
Braintree   781-380-3655
Saugus   781-231-4711

Borders locations:
Framingham   508-875-2321
Chestnut Hill   617-630-1120
Braintree   781-356-5111
Shrewsbury   508-845-8665
North Attleboro 508-699-7766

Music

Music Together
Classes offered: Music classes for infants, toddlers & preschoolers-songs, instrument play, creative movement and dance.
Locations: Bedford & Concord
Classes held at:
First Parish Church, 75 Great Road (Rt.62/Rt.225/Rt.4), Bedford
And
First Parish Church, 2 Lexington Road, Concord
Major Routes/Cross Streets: see above
Phone: Bedford, Concord 978-369-5723
Parking: parking lot
Ages: 0-4
Website: www.musictogether.com
Available for parties: n/a
Discounts: sibling discount
Notes:_____

Music Together

Classes offered: Music classes for infants, toddlers & preschoolers-songs, instrument play, creative movement and dance.

Locations: Lexington, Winchester

Classes held at:

First Baptist Church, 1580 Massachusetts Avenue, Lexington

And

First Congregational Church, 21 Church Street, Winchester

Major Routes/Cross Streets: see above

Phone: Lexington, Winchester 781-402-0906

Parking: parking lot

Ages: 0-4

Website: www.musictogether.com

Or www.joyfulmusic.com

Available for parties: call

Discounts: sibling discount

Notes:_____

Grace Chapel School of Creative Arts

Classes offered: Kindermusik classes, Theater production and workshops, Musical theater (teens), Children's choirs (ages 6-18), Private Lessons in Piano, voice, guitar, brass, winds & strings.

Location: 59 Worthen Road, Lexington

Major Routes/Cross Streets: Rt.4/Rt.225/Massachusetts Avenue

Phone: 781-862-4505 or 781-862-6499

Parking: parking lot

Ages: 0-14

Website: no

Available for parties: n/a

Discounts: n/a

Notes:_____

Music Connection

Classes offered: Kindermusic, exploring music, piano, guitar, drums, saxophone, clarinet, flute, violin

Location: 38 Enon St., #R, Beverly

Major Routes/Cross Streets: Rt.1A
Phone: 978-921-7997
Parking: parking area
Ages: 0-14
Website: www.kidsworks.net
Available for parties: yes
Discounts: no
Notes:_____

<u>**Piano Studio**</u>
Classes offered: piano
Location: 285 East Main St.,
Gloucester
Major Routes/Cross Streets:
Rt.128/Rt.127
Phone: 978-281-1891
Parking: street parking
Ages: 5-14
Website: no
Available for parties: no
Discounts: no
Notes: _all private lessons_____

Don Carr Drum Shop
Classes offered: vocal, drums, guitar, keyboard, saxophone, clarinet, flute
Location: 13 Main St. Rear, Peabody
Major Routes/Cross Streets: Rt.128/Summit Street/Lowell Street
Phone: 978-531-9262
Parking: parking lot
Ages: 5+
Website: no
Available for parties: no
Discounts: no
Notes:_____

Amesbury Art Works
Classes offered: piano, guitar, cello, flute, clarinet, music & art
Location: 10 R Street, Amesbury
Major Routes/Cross Streets: Rt. 150
Phone: 978-388-5954
Parking: parking lot
Ages: call
Website: no
Available for parties: no
Discounts: n/a

Notes:_____

Donovan Music Studios

Classes offered: piano, organ, voice, guitar, strings. Kindermusic, music for little Mozarts and more

Location: 147 South Main St., Bradford

Major Routes/Cross Streets: Rt.495/R.97/Rt.110

Phone: 978-373-9395

Parking: parking area

Ages: 4-14

Website: no

Available for parties: no

Discounts: some-call

Notes:_____

European School of Music

Classes offered: piano lessons

Location: 7 Lawrence Drive, Marblehead

Major Routes/Cross Streets: Rt.129

Phone: 781-631-6676

Parking: street parking

Ages: 5-11

Website: no

Available for parties: no

Discounts: n/a
Notes:_____

Antonelli Music Center
Classes offered: guitar, bass, piano, drums
Location: 143 Main St., North Andover
Major Routes/Cross Streets: Rt.495/Merrimack Street/Water Street
Phone: 978-975-8551
Parking: street parking, parking lot
Ages: 5+
Website: www.antonellimusiccenter.com
Available for parties: no
Discounts: family discounts
Notes:_____

Antionette Perrone Piano Instruction
Classes offered: piano
Location: 185 Massachusetts Ave., North Andover
Major Routes/Cross Streets: Rt.495/Waverly Road
Phone: 978-682-6677

Parking: street parking
Ages: call
Website: no
Available for parties: no
Discounts: no
Notes:_____

The Music Place Inc.
Classes offered: guitar, bass, drums, woodwinds, brass, piano, violin and cello
Location: 41 Main St., North Reading
Major Routes/Cross Streets: Rt.28
Phone: 978-664-6213
Parking: parking lot
Ages: 6+
Website: www.themusicplace.com
Available for parties: no
Discounts: no
Notes: _private lessons, instrument rentals available_____

Timeline Music
Classes offered: piano, violin, woodwinds, brass, and more
Location: 337 North Ave., Wakefield
Major Routes/Cross Streets: Rt.128
Phone: 781-246-4424
Parking: street parking, parking lot in rear
Ages: 7-14
Website: www.timeline4music.com
Available for parties: no
Discounts: no
Notes:_____

Sarrin Music Studio
Classes offered: guitar, bass, drums, vocals, strings, woodwinds
Location: 1098 Main St., Wakefield
Major Routes/Cross Streets: Rt.128/North Avenue/ Church Street
Phone: 781-245-2200
Parking: street parking
Ages: 6+ generally
Website: no
Available for parties: no
Discounts: family discounts

Notes:_____

Performance Music Center
Classes offered: guitar, drums
Location: 405 Main St., Woburn
Major Routes/Cross Streets: Rt.38
Phone: 781-938-6411
Parking: parking lot
Ages: 7-14
Website:
www.performancemusiccenter.com
Available for parties: no
Discounts: no
Notes:_____

Action Music Center
Classes offered: violin, strings,
guitar, drums
Location: 140 Main St., Acton
Phone: 978-263-9288
Major Routes/Cross Streets: Rt.2
Parking: street parking
Ages: 7-14
Website: no
Available for parties: no
Discounts: no
Notes:_____

Indian Hill Music Center

Classes offered: Kindermusic, musical story-hour, music time, piano, recorder, flute, pennywhistle
Location: 36 King St., Littleton
Phone: 978-486-0540
Major Routes/Cross Streets: Rt.2A/Rt.110
Parking: parking lot
Ages: 0-14
Website: www.indianhillmusic.org
Available for parties: no
Discounts: n/a
Notes: _Ensembles available_

Music for Little Mozarts
Classes offered: Piano classes
Location: Steinert's Pianos, Route 9, Sherwood Plaza, Natick
Phone: 508-655-7373
Major Routes/Cross Streets: Rt.9
Parking: parking lot
Ages: 4-6 years
Website: www.msteinert.com
Available for parties: no
Discounts: no
Notes: piano rentals may also be available

Franklin School for Performing Arts
Classes offered: wee play, Kindermusik, piano, voice, woodwinds, violin, guitar, drums. Classes are generally after school and there are many performance opportunities.
Location: 38 Main Street, Franklin
Major Route/Cross Streets: Rt. 140
Phone: 508-528-8668

Parking: street parking
Ages: 2.5-14
Website: www.FSPAonline.com
Available for parties: No
Discounts: N/A
Notes: _____

Music Together
Classes offered: Music classes for infants, toddlers & preschoolers-songs, instrument play, creative movement and dance.
Locations: 165 Main Street, Medway
Major Routes/Cross Streets: Rt.109
Phone: 508-634-3917
Parking: at Telamon Community Center
Ages: 0-4
Website: no
Available for parties: no
Discounts: early payment discounts, multiple session discounts
Notes:_____

Performing Arts Center-Metrowest

Classes offered: Kindermusik, violin, chamber music, jazz, voice, creative dance, songwriting and more!

Location: 140 Pearl Street, Framingham

Major Routes/Cross Streets: Rt.126/Rt.135

Phone: 508-875-5554

Parking: street parking

Ages: 2-14

Website: www.framingham.com/org/mwpac.htm

Available for parties: yes

Discounts: members, multi-class discounts

Notes:_____

Robinson's Music Co.

Classes offered: Beginner Piano lessons

Location: 108 Milk Street, Westboro

Major Routes/Cross Streets: Rt.9/Rt.135

Phone: 508-366-7007

Parking: parking lot

Ages: 5-9 years
Website: www.robinsonmusicinc.com
Available for parties: no
Discounts: family discounts
Notes: Online school pick-up and delivery for rental repairs, exchanges and returns. Also, 4 week trial period for lessons.

Rivers Music School
Classes offered: music & movement, music theory, violin, cello, chorus, guitar, piano, voice, orchestral instruments and more
Location: 333 Winter Street, Weston
Phone: 781-235-6840
Major Routes/Cross Streets: Rt.9/Bogle Street
Parking: parking lot
Ages: 2-14
Website: www.rivers.org
Available for parties: no
Discounts: no
Notes:_____

All Newton Music School Inc.
Classes offered: music & play, joy of music, orchestra, recorders, guitar, kinder keyboard, instrument lab, voice, musical theater "club"
Location: 321 Chestnut St., West Newton
Phone: 617-527-4553
Major Routes/Cross Streets: Rt.90
Parking: very limited parking in lot
Ages: 20 months – 13 years
Website: www.newtonarts.com/id11.htm
Available for parties: no
Discounts: in some cases
Notes:_____

Needham Music
Classes offered: piano, guitar, drums, woodwinds, and more
Location: 947 Great Plain Ave., Needham
Major Routes/Cross Streets: Rt.128
Phone: 781-444-6429
Parking: street parking
Ages: 5-14
Website: www.needhammusic.com

Available for parties: no
Discounts: n/a
Notes:_____

Apple Tree Arts
Classes offered: "Tots and Tunes", "Tiny tunes", Musicgarten, violin, composition, flute, guitar and more
Location: Evangelical Congregational Church, 30 Grafton Common, Grafton
Major Routes/Cross Streets: Rt.140
Phone: 508-839-4286
Parking: parking lot
Ages: 0-14
Website: www.appletreearts.org
Available for parties: no
Discounts: n/a
Notes:_____

Apple Tree Arts
Classes offered: "Tots and Tunes", "Tiny tunes", Musicgarten, violin, composition, flute, guitar and more.
Location: First United Methodist Church, 120 W. Main Street, Westboro

Major Routes/Cross Streets:
Rt.90/Rt.30
Phone: 508-839-4286
Parking: parking lot
Ages: 0-14
Website: www.appletreearts.org
Available for parties: no
Discounts: n/a
Notes:_____

Apple Tree Arts
Classes offered: "Tots and Tunes",
"Tiny tunes", Musicgarten, violin,
composition, flute, guitar and more
Location: The 1830 School House,
Church Road, Shrewsbury
Major Routes/Cross Streets:
Rt.140
Phone: 508-839-4286
Parking: parking lot
Ages: 0-14
Website: www.appletreearts.org
Available for parties: no
Discounts: n/a
Notes:_____

Suzuki Institute of Boston

Classes offered: Instruction of suzuki method violin, cello and flute as well as singing classes. Violin from age 3, flute and pennywhistle from age 5.

Location: 437 Cherry Street, West Newton

Major Routes/Cross Streets: Rt.90/Waltham Street

Phone: 617-566-0020

Parking: parking lot with meters

Ages: 3-14

Website: www.suzukiboston.com

Available for parties: no

Discounts: sliding scale -call

Notes: individual and group lessons. Located in Boston Chinese Cultural Association building.

Milford Performing Arts Center

Classes offered: various music classes

Location: 16 Windsor Road, Milford

Major Routes/Cross Streets: Rt.495/South Street

Phone: 508-473-1684

Parking: parking lot

Ages: call
Website:
www.milford.ma/mpac.htm
Available for parties: n/a
Discounts: n/a
Notes: _summer workshops
too_____

<u>New England Piano</u>
Classes offered: piano lessons
Location: 118 Concord St.,
Framingham
Major Routes/Cross Streets: Rt.
126/Rt.135
Phone: 508-879-4404
Parking: street parking
Ages: call
Website:
www.newenglandpiano.com
Available for parties: no
Discounts: n/a
Notes:_____

Centre Music House
Classes offered: piano, guitar, bass, cello, violin, clarinet, drums, saxophone, trumpet, trombone, violin and voice
Location: 18 Main St., Framingham
Major Routes/Cross Streets: Rt.30/Rt.9
Phone: 508-875-0909
Parking: parking lot located on the side and rear of the building
Ages: 5-14
Website: www.centremusic.com
Available for parties: no
Discounts: family discounts
Notes: Summer "Rock and Blues Band" for teens and pre-teens_____

Franklin School of Performing Arts
Classes offered: wee-play, Kindermusik, voice, composition, theory, guitar, piano, strings and brass
Location: 38 Main St., Franklin
Major Routes/Cross Streets: Rt.140
Phone: 508-528-8668

Parking: street parking
Ages: 2.5-14
Website: www.FSPAonline.com
Available for parties: no
Discounts: n/a
Notes:_____

School of Creative Arts
Classes offered: piano, voice, guitar, bass, violin, cello, recorder, flute, clarinet, saxophone and more
Location: 100 Winter Street, Weston
Major Routes/Cross Streets: Rt.9/Bogle Street
Phone: 978-597-3018
Parking: parking lot
Ages: 5-9
Website: no
Available for parties: no
Discounts: n/a
Notes:_____

Creative Kids
Classes offered: music appreciation
Location: 143 Union Street, Holliston
Major Routes/Cross Streets: Rt.126/Rt.16
Phone: 508-429-8287
Parking: street parking
Ages: 4-6
Website: no
Available for parties: no
Discounts: n/a
Notes:_____

School of Creative Arts
Classes offered: piano, voice, guitar, bass, violin, cello, recorder, flute, clarinet, saxophone and more
Location: Hope International Church, 21 Bruce Rd., Waltham
Major Routes/Cross Streets: Rt.20
Phone: 978-597-3018
Parking: parking lot
Ages: 5-9
Website: no
Available for parties: no
Discounts: n/a
Notes:_____

Music Together

Classes offered: songs, movement, dance, instrument play
Location: 2 Evergreen Lane, Unit 4 (Hopedale Business Park), Hopedale Call for class locations
Major Routes/Cross Streets: see above
Phone: 508-634-3917
Parking: parking lot
Ages: 0-4
Website: www.musictogether.com
Available for parties: n/a
Discounts: n/a
Notes:_____

The Music House

Classes offered: guitar, bass, drums, piano, voice, violin
Location: 157 Main St., Milford
Major Routes/Cross Streets: Rt. 109/Rt.16
Phone: 508-634-8703
Parking: parking lot
Ages: 3-14
Website: www.musichouseweb.com
Available for parties: no

Discounts: family discounts
Notes:_____

Music Together of Newton
Classes offered: songs, movement, dance and instrument play
Location: Trinity Church, 11 Homer Street, Newton Center
Major Routes/Cross Streets: Rt.30
Phone: 617-928-0190
Parking: street parking
Ages: 0-4
Website: www.musictogethernewton.com
Available for parties: n/a
Discounts: n/a
Notes:_____

South Shore Music Conservatory

Classes offered: music for mom/dad & me, joy of music, guitar fun, ensemble music, voice, violin, piano, cello, flute, guitar, pennywhistle and more
Location: 64 Saint Georges St., Duxbury (Ellison Center for the Arts)
Major Routes/Cross Streets: Rt.3/Rt.139
Phone: 781-934-2731
Parking: parking lot
Ages: 0-14
Website: www.southshoreconservatory.org
Available for parties: no
Discounts: n/a
Notes: _many summer programs including musical theater workshops and chamber music academy_

Gymboree
Classes offered: music and play classes
Location: 31 Schoosett Brick Kiln Place, Pembroke
Major Routes/Cross Streets: Rt.3/Rt.53
Phone: 781-826-3665
Parking: parking lot
Ages: 0-5
Website: www.gymboree.com
Available for parties: yes
Discounts: no
Notes:_____

Halifax Music
Classes offered: piano, guitar, musical crafts, woodwinds, drums, intro to music, music instrument exploration, music theory, performing choir, musical theater and more
Location: 284 Plymouth St., Plymouth
Major Routes/Cross Streets: Rt.44
Phone: 781-294-7900
Parking: parking lot
Ages: 3-14

Website: www.halifaxmusic.net
Available for parties: no
Discounts: n/a
Notes:_____

South Shore Conservatory
Classes offered: music for mom/dad & me, joy of music, guitar fun, ensemble music, voice, violin, piano, cello, flute, guitar, pennywhistle and more
Location: 1 Conservatory Drive, Hingham
Major Routes/Cross Streets: Rt.3A/ Fort Hill Street/Beal Street
Phone: 781-749-7565
Parking: parking lot
Ages: 0-14
Website: www.southshoreconservatory.org
Available for parties: no
Discounts: n/a
Notes: _many summer programs including musical theater workshops and chamber music academy_____

Horrigan Drum School
Classes offered: drums, guitar, accordian, bagpipe, trombone, piano, voice, music theory, song writing, organ, saxaphone, flute, trumpet and more
Location: 342 Center St., Brockton
Major Routes/Cross Streets: Rt. 123
Phone: 508-588-3786
Parking: parking lot
Ages: 3-14
Website: www.horriganmusicschool.com
Available for parties: no
Discounts: call
Notes: __home lessons available too_____

Central Music Store
Classes offered: guitar, bass, flute, clarinet, saxophone, piano, drums, voice, trumpet, trombone, violin
Location: 685 Pleasant Street, Brockton
Major Routes/Cross Streets: Rt.24/ Rt.27
Phone: 781-740-8863

Parking: parking lot
Ages: 6-14 generally
Website:
www.centralmusicstore.com
Available for parties: no
Discounts: no
Notes:_____

Boston Guitar Works
Classes offered: guitar
Location: 1997 Main St., Brockton
Major Routes/Cross Streets:
Rt.123
Phone: 508-580-0088
Parking: parking lot
Ages: 5-14
Website: www.bostonguitar.com
Available for parties: no
Discounts: n/a
Notes:_____

South Shore Music Co.
Classes offered: guitar, bass, piano,
drums, voice, clarinet
Location: 13 Washington St.,
Weymouth
Major Routes/Cross Streets: Rt.53
Phone: 781-331-3333

Parking: parking lot and street parking
Ages: 7-14
Website: www.justplaymusic.com/lessons.html
Available for parties: no
Discounts: no
Notes:_____

Stoughton Music Center
Classes offered: piano, drums, guitar, voice, woodwinds, strings, brass and more
Location: 968 Washington St., #2, Stoughton
Major Routes/Cross Streets: Rt.138
Phone: 781-344-8772
Parking: parking lot
Ages: 5-14
Website: www.stoughtonmusic.com/musicschool.html
Available for parties: no
Discounts: no
Notes:_____

Nature & Science

Drumlin Farm
Classes offered: owls & birds, maple sugaring, sheep sheering
Location: 208 South Great Road, Lincoln
Major Routes/Cross Streets: Rt.117
Phone: 781-259-9807
Parking: parking lot
Ages: 0-14 generally- some programs may have other age requirements
Website: www.lincoln-ma.com/town_groups/drumlin.htm
Available for parties: no
Discounts: members
Notes:_____

Joppa Flats
Classes offered: nature, animals
Location: Rolfe's Lane, Newburyport Plum Island/Parker River Refuge
Major Routes/Cross Streets: Rt.95/Rt.113/Rolfe's Lane
Phone: 978-462-9998
Parking: parking lot
Ages: 4-14 generally- some programs may have other age requirements
Website: www.massaudubon.org
Available for parties: n/a
Discounts: members
Notes:_____

Ipswich River
Classes offered: explorers, nature workshops, nature & art, river ecology, art
Location: 87 Perkins Row, Topsfield
Major Routes/Cross Streets: Rt.95/Rt.1/Rt.97
Phone: 978-887-9264
Parking: parking lot

Ages: 4-14 generally- some programs may have other age requirements
Website: www.massaudubon.org
Available for parties: n/a
Discounts: members
Notes:_____

Habitat Education Center

Classes offered: Eco-safari, habitats, explorers, Kindercamp, twilight camp and more
Location: 10 Juniper Road, Belmont
Major Routes/Cross Streets: Rt.2/Clifton Street
Phone: 617-489-5050
Parking: parking lot
Ages: 5-14
Website: www.massaudubon.org
Available for parties: see below
Discounts: members
Notes: _Georgian style estate with wonderful gardens is also available for rental_____

Western Suburbs

Broadmoor Wildlife Sanctuary
Classes offered: birds, astronomy, animal tracking, owls
Location: 280 Eliot Street, Natick
Major Routes/Cross Streets: Rt.16
Phone: 508-655-2296
Parking: parking lot
Ages: 5-14 generally
Website: www.massaudubon.org
Available for parties: n/a
Discounts: members
Notes:_____

Garden in the Woods
Classes offered: craft classes, nature, animals, insects, science, astronomy, hikes, birds
Location: 180 Hemingway Road, Framingham
Major Routes/Cross Streets: Rt.30/Edgell Road
Phone: 508-237-4924
Parking: parking lot
Ages: 5-10 generally
Website:
www.gardeninthewoods.org

Available for parties: n/a
Discounts: members
Notes:_____

Stony Brook Reservation
Classes offered: animals, habitats, insects, fish, frogs, Eco-art, crafts, snakes, butterflies and more
Location: North Street, Norfolk
Major Routes/Cross Streets: Rt.495/Rt.1A/Rt.115
Phone: 508-528-3140
Parking: parking lot
Ages: 4-14
Website: www.massaudubon.org
Available for parties: yes
Discounts: members
Notes: summer camp too!_____

North River
Classes offered: pre-school stories, little look-abouts, explorers, naturalist series, river adventures (kayak)
Location: 2000 Main Street, Marshfield
Major Routes/Cross Streets: Rt.3/Rt.53/Rt.3A
Phone: 781-837-9400
Parking: parking lot
Ages: 3-14
Website: www.massaudubon.org
Available for parties: n/a
Discounts: members
Notes:_____

Oak Knoll
Classes offered: nature, insects, art projects
Location: 1417 Park Street, Attleboro
Major Routes/Cross Streets: Rt.95/Rt.123
Phone: 508-223-3060
Parking: parking lot

Ages: 3-14 generally
Website: www.massaudubon.org
Available for parties: n/a
Discounts: members
Notes:_____

Visual Arts Center
Classes offered: drawing
Location: 963 Washington St.,
Canton
Major Routes/Cross Streets:
Rt.93/Rt.138
Phone: 781-821-8853
Parking: parking lot
Ages: varies- call
Website: www.massaudubon.org
Available for parties: n/a
Discounts: members
Notes:_____

Moose Hill Wildlife Sanctuary
Classes offered: habitats, crafts,
insects, art, adventure series, start
& space, trekkers and more
Location: 293 Moose Hill Street,
Sharon
Major Routes/Cross Streets:
Rt.95/Rt.1

Phone: 781-784-5691
Parking: parking lot
Ages: 4-14
Website: www.massaudubon.org
Available for parties: n/a
Discounts: members
Notes:_____

South Shore Natural Science Center

Classes offered: nature, environmental, animals, reptiles, science, birds, owls, bats, maple sugaring, and habitats
Location: Jacobs Lane, Norwell
Major Routes/Cross Streets: Rt.3/Rt.123
Phone: 781-659-2559
Parking: parking lot
Ages: 3.5-14
Website: www.ssnsc.org
Available for parties? Yes
Discounts: members
Notes: _school vacation programs too_____

MDC Blue Hills Reservation & South Region Sites.

Classes offered: astronomy, nature exploration and animals.

Location: classes are in several locations: Blue Hill, Houghton's Pond, Bunker Hill Quarry, etc. Call for details.

Major Routes/Cross Streets: varies

Phone: 617-698-1802

Parking: free parking in lot

Ages: 5-9 generally

Website: www.state.ma.us/mdc/blue.htm

Available for parties: N/A

Discounts: members

Notes:_____

SPORTS

This section is divided into sub-categories:

Northern Suburbs

Guard Up
Classes offered: Youth tactical games, fencing
Location: 16A Garfield Circle, Burlington
Major Routes/Cross Streets: Rt.128
Phone: 781-270-4800
Parking: parking in small lot and street parking
Ages: 6-14
Website: www.guardup.com
Available for parties: yes
Discounts: n/a
Notes:_____

Western Suburbs

Teamworks Sports Center
Classes offered: Soccer, basketball, football, hockey, gymnastics, outdoor adventure and even Circus arts.

Location: Otis Street, Northboro (on the Northboro/Westboro line)
Major Routes/Cross Streets: Rt. 9
Phone: 508-351-9800
Parking: Free parking in lot
Ages: 3 to 14
Website: www.teamworkscenters.com
Available for parties: Yes
Discounts: sibling discounts
Notes: indoor facility, school break camps available

Newton Indoor Sports
Classes offered: roller hockey, soccer
Location: 125 Wells Ave, Newton
Major Routes/Cross Streets: Rt.128/Hunting Road
Phone: 617-964-0400
Parking: parking lot
Ages: 4-14
Website: www.newtonindoorsports.com
Available for parties: yes
Discounts: n/a
Notes:

The Habitat for Soccer & Sports
Classes offered: soccer, sports, baseball/softball, football, basketball
Location: 374 West St., Uxbridge
Major Routes/Cross Streets: Rt.16/Rt.146
Phone: 508-278-9888
Parking: parking lot
Ages: 6+
Website: www.thehab.com
Available for parties: YES
Discounts: 10% sibling discount
Notes: _Sports leagues and camps too_____

Longfellow Sports Club
Classes offered: Swimming, sports (soccer, basketball) martial arts
Location: 203 Oak St, Natick
Major Routes/Cross Streets: Rt.9
Phone: 508-653-4633 ext.217
Parking: parking lot
Ages: 3.5-14
Website: www.longellowclubs.com
Available for parties: yes
Discounts: n/a

Notes: <u>"kid's night out" pizza parties</u>
<u>too</u>

John Smith Sports Center
Classes offered: soccer
Location: 10 Sumner Street, Milford
Major Routes/Cross Streets: Rt.
85
Phone: 508-634-8080
Parking: free parking in lot
Ages: 4-14
Website: no
Available for parties: yes
Discounts: n/a
Notes:

Gymboree
Classes offered: Active play
programs with parent participation.
Locations: Rt. 9, Westboro
Major Routes/Cross Streets: Rt.
9/Otis Street.
Phone: 508-366-1495
Parking: Free parking in lot
Ages: 0-4
Website: <u>www.gymboree.com</u>
Available for parties: YES
Discounts: none

Notes:_____

Southern Suburbs

Dedham Health & Athletic Club
Classes offered: rock climbing, swimming lessons, gymnastics
Location: 200 Providence Highway, Dedham
Major Routes/Cross Streets: Rt.1
Phone: 781-326-2900
Parking: Free parking in lot
Ages: 6 months-14 years
Website: www.dedhamhealth.com
Available for parties: yes
Discounts: n/a
Notes:_____

Northern Suburbs

Westford Racquet & Fitness Club
Classes offered: swimming
Location: 4 Littleton Road, Westford
Major Routes/Cross Streets:
Rt.110
Phone: 978-692-7597
Parking: free parking in lot
Ages: 6 months -14
Website: n/a
Available for parties: n/a
Discounts: n/a
Notes:_____

Harvard Ridge Pool Club
Classes offered: swimming lessons
Location: 90 Swanson Road,
Boxborough
Major Routes/Cross Streets:
Rt.495/Rt.111
Phone: 978-263-3700
Parking: parking lot
Ages: 9 months -14
Website: www.harvardridgepool.com
Available for parties: n/a

Discounts: n/a
Notes: _classes available to non-members_____

Suburban Athletic Club
Classes offered: Swimming classes, "Tumble and Splash", "Scuba rangers".
Location: 10 Roxanna Street, Framingham
Major Routes/Cross Streets: Rt. 135/Rt. 126
Phone: 508-879.6544
Parking: Free parking in lot.
Ages: infant to 14 depending on class
Website: www.suburbanalthltic.com
Available for parties: YES
Discounts: N/A
Notes:_____

Longfellow Sports Club
Classes offered: Swimming
Location: 203 Oak St, Natick
Major Routes/Cross Streets: Rt.9
Phone: 508-653-4633 ext.217
Parking: parking lot
Ages: 3.5-14
Website: www.longfellowclubs.com
Available for parties: yes

Discounts: call
Notes:_____

Wayside Racquet & Swim Club

Classes offered: swimming lessons
Location: 80 Broadmeadow Road, Marlboro
Major Routes/Cross Streets:
Rt.85/Boston Post Road
Phone: 508-481-1797
Parking: parking lot
Ages: 6 months- 14
Website: www.wayside.net
Available for parties: yes
Discounts: n/a
Notes: __Youth swim team too.

Raynham Athletic Club

Classes offered: swimming lessons
Location: 1250 Route 44, Raynham
Major Routes/Cross Streets: Rt.44
Phone: 508-823-5440
Parking: parking lot
Ages: 2-12
Website:
www.raynhamathleticclub.com
Available for parties: yes
Discounts: n/a
Notes: ___Kids club memberships available_____

Dedham Health & Athletic Club

Classes offered: Swimming lessons
Location: 200 Providence Highway, Dedham
Major Routes/Cross Streets: Rt. 1
Phone: 781-326-2900
Parking: free parking in lot
Ages: 6 months-14
Website: www.dedhamhealth.com
Available for parties: yes
Discounts: n/a
Notes:_____

Absolute Yoga
Classes offered: Yoga for kids & pre-teens
Location: 50 West Main St., Hopkinton
Major Routes/Cross Streets: Rt. 85
Phone: 508-625-1152
Parking: free parking in lot
Ages: generally 6+
Website: www.absoluteyoga.net
Available for parties: N/A
Discounts: N/A
Notes: located in Golden Pond

Dedham Health & Athletic Club
Classes offered: yoga
Location: 200 Providence Highway, Dedham
Major Routes/Cross Streets: Rt. 1
Phone: 781-326-2900
Parking: free parking in lot
Ages: 3 months+
Website: www.dedhamhealth.com

Available for parties: yes
Discounts: n/a
Notes:_____

Sports/Gymnastics

Northern Suburbs

One Stop Fun Inc.
Classes offered: gymnastics, dance, cheerleading
Location: 49 Power Road, Westford
Major Routes/Cross Streets: Rt.495/Rt.2A
Phone: 978-692-9907
Parking: parking lot
Ages: 12 months (walking)-14
Website: www.onestopfun.com
Available for parties: yes
Discounts: siblings of gymnastics students can attend gymania free during gymnastics
Notes: _vacation camps and team camps too_____

Ace Gymnastics

Classes offered: gymnastics (mom & me, tumble bears, up to recreational teams)

Location: 91 Newbury Port Turnpike, Ipswich (Ipswich Industrial Park)

Major Routes/Cross Streets: Rt.1

Phone: 978-356-8332

Parking: parking lot

Ages: 1-14

Website: www.acegymnasticsinc.com

Available for parties: n/a

Discounts: n/a

Notes: _end of year shows_____

Iron Rail Gymnastics Academy

Classes offered: gymnastics (mom &me, boys & girls recreational, teams)

Location: 91 Grapevine Road, Wenham

Major Routes/Cross Streets: Rt.128

Phone: 978-468-9544

Parking: parking lot

Ages: 1.5-14

Website: www.ironrail.com
Available for parties: yes
Discounts: n/a
Notes: private lessons available, vacation camps too.

Reading Gymnastics Academy
Classes offered: gymnastics (playgym, junior gymnast, gymnast, boys tumbling, teams, cheerleading)
Location: 172 Woburn St., Reading
Major Routes/Cross Streets: Rt.28/Rt.129
Phone: 781-944-2277
Parking: parking lot
Ages: 1-14
Website: www.readinggymnastics.com
Available for parties: n/a
Discounts: family discounts
Notes:

Tops USA Gymnastics
Classes offered: gymnastics (tumbling, cheerleading, boys and girls recreational, teams)
Location: 4 Hancock St., Woburn

Major Routes/Cross Streets:
Rt.38/Salem Street
Phone: 781-935-8825
Parking: parking lot
Ages: 3-14
Website:
www.eteamz.com/sites/topsusa/
Available for parties: yes
Discounts: n/a
Notes: _Private lessons available____

<u>Gymnastics & More</u>
Classes offered: gymnastics
Location: 8 Micro Drive, Woburn
Major Routes/Cross Streets:
Rt.128/Winn Street/Montvale
Avenue
Phone: 781-938-3669
Parking: parking lot
Ages: 1.5 - 14
Website: www.gymandmore.com
Available for parties: yes
Discounts: family discounts
Notes:_____

Absolute Gymnastics Academy

Classes offered: gymnastics (Tumbletime, kindergarten tumbling, boys and girls recreational, development programs, competitive teams)
Location: 87 Progress Ave., Tyngsboro
Major Routes/Cross Streets: Rt.3/Rt.113/Cummings Road
Phone: 978-649-7722
Parking: parking lot
Ages: 18 months -12
Website: www.absolutegymnastics.com
Available for parties: yes
Discounts: n/a
Notes:_____

Planet Gymnastics

Classes offered: gymnastics
Location: 10 Granite Road, Acton
Major Routes/Cross Streets: Rt.128/Rt.2/Rt.119
Phone: 978-263-1900
Parking: parking lot
Ages: 2.5-14

Website: www.planet-gymnastics.com
Available for parties: yes
Discounts: n/a
Notes:_____

Gymboree Play Programs
Classes offered: gym(babies, walkers, toddlers, gym pairs)
Location: 279 Cambridge St., Burlington
Major Routes/Cross Streets: Rt.3A
Phone: 781-229-1886
Parking: parking lot
Ages: 0-4
Website: www.gymboree.com
Available for parties: yes
Discounts: none
Notes:_____

Sola's Gymnastic Academy
Classes offered: gymnastics
Location: 49 Uxbridge Road, Mendon
Major Routes/Cross Streets: Rt. 140
Phone: 508-634-0012
Parking: Free parking in lot
Ages: 2-14
Website: none
Available for parties: YES
Discounts: sibling discounts
Notes:_____

Gymnastics Learning Center
Classes offered: gymnastics, gym & swim, play programs, cheerleading
Location: 574 Lake St., Shrewsbury
Major Routes/Cross Streets: Rt.9/Lake Street
Phone: 508-792-1551
Parking: parking lot
Ages: 12 months (walkers) - 14
Website: no
Available for parties: YES
Discounts: n/a

Notes:_____

Creative Movement and Arts Center
Classes offered: Gymnastics, Dance
Location: 145 Rosemary Street, Needham
Major Routes/Cross Streets: Rt.128/Highland Avenue
Phone: 781-449-2707
Parking: parking lot
Ages: 3 months – 10 years depending on program
Website: www.brighthorizons.com/creativemo vement/
Available for parties: yes
Discounts: family discounts
Notes:_____

Massachusetts Gymnastics Center
Classes offered: Gymnastics programs.
Locations: 108 Clematis Ave., Waltham
Major Routes/Cross Streets: Rt.128/Totten Pond Road/Lexington Street

Phone: 781-893-2009
Parking: parking lot
Ages: 2-14
Website: www.massgymnastics.com
Available for parties: Yes
Discounts: family discounts, multiple class discounts
Notes:_____

Creative Movement and Arts Center

Classes offered: Gymnastics, Dance
Location: 56C Union Avenue, Sudbury
Major Routes/Cross Streets: Rt.20
Phone: 978-440-7554
Parking: parking lot
Ages: 3 months- 10 years
Website: www.brighthorizons.com/creativemovement
Available for parties: yes
Discounts: family discounts
Notes:_____

The Gymnastic Place
Classes offered: Gymnastics
Location: 19 Depot Street, 2nd floor, Uxbridge
Major Routes/Cross Streets: Rt.122/Mendon Street
Phone: 508-234-5565
Parking: parking lot
Ages: call
Website: www.indiepro.com/gymnastics
Available for parties: yes
Discounts: n/a
Notes: dance and yoga too_____

Massachusetts Gymnastics Center
Classes offered: Gymnastics programs.
Locations: 74 Otis Street, Westboro
Major Routes/Cross Streets: Rt. 9
Phone: 508-870-0253
Parking: Free parking in lot
Ages: 2-14
Website: www.massgymnastics.com
Available for parties: Yes
Discounts: family discounts, multiple class discount
Notes:_____

Exxcel
Classes offered: Gymnastics, Climbing, Tumbling and Fitness Programs
Location: 60 Kendrick Street, Needham
Major Routes/Cross Streets: Rt.95/128
Phone: 781-453-2220
Parking: parking lot
Ages: 18 months - 14
Website: www.exxcel.net
Available for parties: YES
Discounts: sibling discounts
Notes: year end show, summer camp too

The Little Gym
Classes offered: gymnastics, pre-school creative movement and teams
Location: Gould's Colonial Plaza, 74 Main St (Rte.109) Medway
Major Routes/Cross Streets: Rt. 109
Phone: 508-533-9405
Parking: parking lot

Ages: 6 months to 12 years
Website: www.tlgmedway.com
Available for parties: YES
Discounts: n/a
Notes: summer camps too, Parent's "survival night" on select Friday/Saturday nights_____

Brestyan's American Gymnastics Club

Classes offered: gymnastics (preschool, beginners, intermediate, advanced, pre-team and team)
Location: 260 Eliot St, Ashland
Major Routes/Cross Streets: Rt.126
Phone: 508-881-7770
Parking: free parking in lot
Ages: 2-13
Website: www.brestyans.com
Available for parties: n/a
Discounts: n/a
Notes:_____

Gymnastics Training Center
Classes offered: gymnastics (preschool, boys classes, recreational and teams)
Location: 16 Everette Road, Holliston
Major Routes/Cross Streets: Rt.16
Phone: 508-429-7779
Parking: Free parking in lot or on street
Ages: 3-14
Website: no
Available for parties: YES
Discounts: each additional child 10% off
Notes: drop in open gym available- call for schedule, summer camp too. End of year gym show!

Sudbury Gymnastics Center
Classes offered: gymnastics (tiny tots, elementary grades, boys classes, teams)
Location: 53 Brigham St. #1, Marlboro
Major Routes/Cross Streets: Rt.495/Rt.20/Rt.85/Mill Street
Phone: 508-485-2255

Parking: parking lot
Ages: 2-14
Website:
www.sudburygymnastics.com
Available for parties: yes
Discounts: family discounts,
multiple class discounts
Notes:_____

Flipside Gymnastics
Classes offered: gymnastics and
specialized programs
Location: 2 Franklin St., Medway
Major Routes/Cross Streets:
Rt.109
Phone: 508-533-2353
Parking: parking in back
Ages: 18 months –14 years
Website: none
Available for parties: N/A
Discounts: sibling discounts,
multiple class discounts
Notes:_____

McKeon Dance & Gymnastics
Classes offered: gymnastics
(preschool, beginner, boys classes,
elementary, cheerleading, teams)

Location: 3 Spaceway Lane, Hopedale (Hopedale-Draper Airport Park)
Major Routes/Cross Streets: South Main Street/Hartford Avenue
Phone: 508-473-8166
Parking: parking lot
Ages: 2-14
Website: www.mckeondancegym.com
Available for parties: n/a
Discounts: n/a
Notes:_____

Jean's School of Gymnastics
Classes offered: gymnastics (funtastics, small-fry, recreational and competitive teams too)
Location: 255 Main St., Marlboro
Major Routes/Cross Streets: Rt.20
Phone: 508-481-4401
Parking: parking lot or street
Ages: 8 months-14 years
Website: www.jeansgymnastics.com
Available for parties: yes
Discounts: family discounts
Notes: summer camp too_____

Quigg's School of Gymnastics
Classes offered: gymnastics (parent & tot, preschool, kindergarten, recreational, tumbling and teams)
Location: 260 Maple Street, Bellingham
Major Routes/Cross Streets: Rt.126/Maple Street
Phone: 508-966-3808
Parking: parking lot
Ages: 18 months- 12 years
Website: www.quiggsgym.com
Available for parties: yes
Discounts: family discounts available
Notes:_____

Planet Gymnastics
Classes offered: gymnastics (tiny tumblers, gymstars, gymgirls & gymboys)
Location: 5 Chrysler Rd., Natick
Major Routes/Cross Streets: Rt. 9
Phone: 508-647-1777
Parking: free parking in lot
Ages: 12 months (walkers) to 12
Website: www.planetgym.com

Available for parties: YES
Discounts: discount for additional classes, discount for siblings
Notes: _Camps too

Gymnastics Express
Classes offered: gymnastics (preschool, recreational, teams, etc.)
Location: 46 Middlesex Ave., Natick
Major Routes/Cross Streets: Rt.135/Spring Street
Phone: 508-650-1662
Parking: parking lot
Ages: 3-14
Website: www.gymnasticsexpress.com
Available for parties: yes
Discounts: n/a
Notes:_____

Southern Suburbs

Walpole Gymnastics Academy
Classes offered: gymnastics (toddler gym, non-competitive groups and teams)
Location: 10 Merchants Dr., Walpole
Major Routes/Cross Streets: Rt.1A/Norfolk Street
Phone: 508-668-9688
Parking: parking lot
Ages: 2-14
Website: no
Available for parties: yes
Discounts: n/a
Notes: <u>kids night out on Friday nights</u>_____

Massachusetts Gymnastics Center
Classes offered: Gymnastics programs (tumble tots, preschool, boys and girls classes.)
Locations: 4 Keith Way, Hingham
Major Routes/Cross Streets: Rt.53/Derby Street
Phone: 781-740-8748
Parking: parking lot

Ages: 2-14
Website: www.massgymnastics.com
Available for parties: Yes
Discounts: family discount, multiple class discounts
Notes:_____

Gymnastic Academy of Boston

Classes offered: Gymnastics, competitive teams, cheering programs
Location: 95 Vanderbilt Ave., Norwood
Major Routes/Cross Streets: Rt.1
Phone: 781-769-6150
Parking: free parking in lot
Ages: 3-14 generally
Website: none
Available for parties: yes
Discounts: n/a
Notes: __open gym times too $5 per child._____

Creative Movement and Arts Center

Classes offered: Gymnastics
Location: 85 West Street, Walpole

Major Routes/Cross Streets:
Rt/1A
Phone: 508-850-9580
Parking: parking lot
Ages: 3 months – 10 years
Website: www.brighthorizons.com/creativemovement
Available for parties: yes
Discounts: family discounts, multiple class discount
Notes:_____

Dedham Health & Athletic Club
Classes offered: gymnastics
Location: 200 Providence Highway, Dedham
Major Routes/Cross Streets: Rt. 1
Phone: 781-326-2900
Parking: free parking in lot
Ages: 6 months – 7 years
Website: www.dedhamhealth.com
Available for parties: yes
Discounts: n/a
Notes: _rock climbing parties too!__

Head over Heels Gymnastics Inc.
Classes offered: gymnastics (tiny-tots, gymkids, girls and boys recreational, teams)
Location: 412 Washington St., Norwell
Major Routes/Cross Streets: Rt.3/Main Street
Phone: 781-659-3378
Parking: parking lot
Ages: 2-14
Website: www.headoverheelsgymnastics.com
Available for parties: yes
Discounts: family discounts, multiple class discounts
Notes:_____

Gymboree of Plymouth
Classes offered: gym play, creative movement
Location: 91 Carver Road, Plymouth
Major Routes/Cross Streets: Rt.44
Phone: 508-830-9626
Parking: parking lot
Ages: 0-4
Website: www.gymboree.com

Available for parties: yes
Discounts: none
Notes:_____

Jungle Gym
Classes offered: gymnastics (gym, boys tumbling, cheerleading)
Location: 620 Bedford St., Bridgewater
Major Routes/Cross Streets: Rt.104/Rt.28/Rt.18
Phone: 508-697-1180
Parking: parking lot
Ages: 10 months- 10 years
Website: www.bridgewaterfitness.com/other.htm
Available for parties: yes
Discounts: n/a
Notes: open gym Tuesday and Thursday_____

Joan's Olympic Gym & Fitness
Classes offered: gymnastics (parent/child, group gym, recreational tumble)
Location: 197 Quincy Ave., Braintree

Major Routes/Cross Streets: Rt.53
Phone: 781-843-9624
Parking: parking lot
Ages: call
Website: www.usa-gymnastics.org/ clubs/ma/027296.htm
Available for parties: n/a
Discounts: n/a
Notes:_____

Sports/Golf

Northern Suburbs

Solomon Pond Golf Center
Classes offered: golf
Location: 317 South St., Berlin
Major Routes/Cross Streets:
Rt.495/Rt.290/Solomon Pond Mall
Road
Phone: 978-838-2333
Parking: parking lot
Ages: 10+
Website: no
Available for parties: n/a
Discounts: package pricing
available
Notes:_____

Swanson Meadows
Classes offered: golf
Location: 216 Rangeway Road,
North Billerica
Major Routes/Cross Streets:
Rt.3A/Rt.129
Phone: 978-670-7777
Parking: parking lot
Ages: 7-14

Website:
www.swansonmeadows.com
Available for parties: n/a
Discounts: package pricing
Notes: _____

Western Suburbs

Pine Crest Golf Club
Classes offered: Golf
Location: 212 Prentice Street, Holliston
Major Routes/Cross Streets: Rt.126, Rt. 16,Highland Ave.
Phone: 508-429-9871
Parking: free parking in lot
Ages: 7+
Website: www.pinecrestgolfclub.org
Available for parties: N/A
Discounts: N/A
Notes: junior golf league for ages 10+ and summer camps too

Golf Teaching Center
Classes offered: golf
Location: 142 School St., Northboro
Major Routes/Cross Streets: Rt.20/Main Street
Phone: 508-351-9500
Parking: parking lot
Ages: 7-14
Website: no
Available for parties: n/a
Discounts: n/a

Notes:_____

Juniper Hill Golf Course
Classes offered: golf
Location: 202 Brigham St., Northboro
Major Routes/Cross Streets: Rt.135
Phone: 508-393-2444
Parking: parking lot
Ages: 7-14
Website: www.junipergc.com
Available for parties: n/a
Discounts: call
Notes: summer programs available_____

East Coast Golf Academy
Classes offered: golf
Location: 333 SW Cutoff, Northboro
Major Routes/Cross Streets: Rt.20
Phone: 508-842-3311
Parking: parking lot
Ages: 10+
Website: www.eastcoastgolf.org
Available for parties: n/a
Discounts: package pricing available

Notes: junior clinics for kids,

Whitinsville Golf Club
Classes offered: golf
Location: 169 Fletcher St.,
Whitinsville
Major Routes/Cross Streets:
Rt.122/Church Street/Douglas
Road
Phone: 508-234-9421
Parking: parking lot
Ages: 7+ (teacher discretion)
Website: no
Available for parties: n/a
Discounts: n/a
Notes: private club but lesson are
available to non-members

Bellingham Golf Learning Center
Classes offered: golf
Location: 191 Mechanic St.,
Bellingham
Major Routes/Cross Streets:
Rt.140
Phone: 508-966-4567
Parking: parking lot
Ages: 7-14
Website: no

Available for parties: n/a
Discounts: no
Notes:_____

<u>Blissful Meadows</u>
Classes offered: golf
Location: 801 Chockalog Street, Uxbridge
Major Routes/Cross Streets: Rt.146/Rt.16
Phone: 508-278-6113
Parking: parking lot
Ages: 5-14
Website: <u>www.blissfulmeadows.com</u>
Available for parties: n/a
Discounts: package discounts
Notes: _junior clinics available_

Southern Suburbs

Ridder Golf Learning Center
Classes offered: golf
Location: 389 Oak Street, East Bridgewater
Major Routes/Cross Streets: Rt.18
Phone: 781-447-6613
Parking: Parking lot
Ages: 5-14
Website: no
Available for parties: n/a
Discounts: n/a
Notes: _summer camps too_____

Norwood Country Club
Classes offered: golf
Location: 400 Providence Highway, Norwood
Major Routes/Cross Streets: Rt.1
Phone: 781-769-5880
Parking: parking lot
Ages: 5-14
Website: no
Available for parties: n/a
Discounts: package discounts

Notes: _no membership required
for lessons_

Sports/Tennis

Northern Suburbs

Willows Racquet & Fitness Center
Classes offered: tennis
Location: 815 Turnpike Street, North Andover
Major Routes/Cross Streets: Rt.114
Phone: 978-687-0505
Parking: parking lot
Ages: 6-14
Website: no
Available for parties: n/a
Discounts: call
Notes: _classes available to non-members_____

Thoreau Club of Concord
Classes offered: tennis
Location: 275 Forest Ridge Road, Concord
Major Routes/Cross Streets: Rt.62
Phone: 978-369-7349
Parking: parking lot
Ages: 8-14
Website: www.thoreau.com

Available for parties: yes
Discounts: n/a
Notes: <u>programs open to members and non-members</u>

Western Suburbs

Tri Valley Tennis Club
Classes offered: tennis (tiny tots, junior development, drills and preparation for tournaments)
Location: 120 Pond Street, Ashland
Major Routes/Cross Streets: Rt.126
Phone: 508-881-7111
Parking: parking lot
Ages: 4-14
Website: www.trivalleytennis.com
Available for parties: n/a
Discounts: n/a
Notes: open to members and non-members

Natick Racquet Club
Classes offered: tennis (little tennis, junior teams)
Location: 16 Michigan Drive, Natick
Major Routes/Cross Streets: Rt.9/Oak Street
Phone: 508-653-4606
Parking: parking lot
Ages: 4+

Website:
www.longfellowclubs.com/natickrac
quetclub.htm
Available for parties: call
Discounts: n/a
Notes: covered during winter,
membership required (junior
memberships available), affiliated
with the Longfellow Club in Wayland

Weston Racquet Club
Classes offered: tennis
Location: 132 West St., Waltham
Major Routes/Cross Streets:
Rt.128
Phone: 781-890-4285
Parking: parking lot
Ages: 5-14
Website:
www.westonracquetclub.com
Available for parties: n/a
Discounts: no
Notes:_____

Wayside Racquet and Swim Club
Classes offered: tennis
Location: 80 Broad Meadow Road,
Marlboro

Major Routes/Cross Streets:
Rt.20/Rt.85
Phone: 508-481-1797
Parking: parking lot
Ages: 5-14
Website: www.wayside.net
Available for parties: n/a
Discounts: none
Notes:_____

Westboro Tennis and Swim Club
Classes offered: tennis
Location: 35 Chauncy St., Westboro
Major Routes/Cross Streets:
Rt.9/Lyman Street
Phone: 508-366-1222
Parking: parking lot
Ages: 4-14
Website: www.westborotennisand
swimclub.com
Available for parties: n/a
Discounts: n/a
Notes:_____

Waltham Athletic Club
Classes offered: tennis
Location: 249 Lexington St. #1,
Waltham

Major Routes/Cross Streets:
Rt.128/Main Street
Phone: 781-899-5000
Parking: parking lot
Ages: 7+
Website: www.walthamathletic.com
Available for parties: yes
Discounts: n/a
Notes: private clinics also available

Southern Suburbs

Dartmouth Indoor Tennis Inc.
Classes offered: tennis
Location: 757 State Road, North Dartmouth
Major Routes/Cross Streets: Rt.6
Phone: 508-993-4811
Parking: parking lot
Ages: call
Website: none
Available for parties: n/a
Discounts: n/a
Notes:_____

Wimbledon 109 Tennis Club
Classes offered: tennis
Location: 20 County Street, Walpole

Major Routes/Cross Streets:
Rt.109
Phone: 508-668-7109
Parking: parking lot
Ages: 7-14
Website: no
Available for parties: n/a
Discounts: none
Notes: __summer clinic
too_____

Weymouth Tennis Club
Classes offered: tennis
Location: 75 Finnell Drive,
Weymouth
Major Routes/Cross Streets:
Rt.3/West Street
Phone: 781-337-4600
Parking: parking lot
Ages: 3-14
Website: www.weymouthclub.com
Available for parties: yes
Discounts: n/a
Notes:_____

Rising Star Equestrian Center
Classes offered: Horseback riding lessons.
Location: 145 Summer Street, Medway
Major Routes/Cross Streets: Rt.126
Phone: 508-533-8551
Parking: parking lot
Ages: 6-14
Website: www.risingstareqctr.com
Available for parties: n/a
Discounts: n/a
Notes:_____

Broad Hill Equestrian Center
Classes offered: Horseback riding lessons
Location: 179 Highland Street, Holliston
Major Routes/Cross Streets: Rt.135/Central Street/ Highland Street
Phone: 508-429-9411
Parking: parking lot
Ages: 6-14

Website: www.broadhill.com
Available for parties: n/a
Discounts: n/a
Notes: Indoor arena as well as outdoor facilities. Private, semi-private and group lessons available

Canton Equestrian Center
Classes offered: Horseback riding lessons
Location: 1095 Randolph St, Canton
Major Routes/Cross Streets: Rt.138
Phone: 781-828-1681
Parking: parking lot
Ages: generally 6-14
Website: www.cantonequestriancenter.com
Discounts: n/a
Available for parties: n/a
Notes: Indoor arena too. Private, semi-private and group lessons available

Northern Suburbs

Bruce McCorry's Martial Arts Academy Inc.
Classes offered: martial arts
Location: 220 Newbury St., Peabody
Major Routes/Cross Streets: Rt.1
Phone: 978-535-7878
Parking: parking lot
Ages: 3-14
Website: www.brucemccorrys.com
Available for parties: no
Discounts: n/a
Notes: summer camp too, after-school programs

North Shore Karate Academy
Classes offered: martial arts
Location: Rt. 110, Salisbury (inside Active Fitness Gym)
Major Routes/Cross Streets: Rt.110
Phone: 978-927-5202
Parking: parking lot
Ages: call

Website:
www.northshorekarate.com
Available for parties: n/a
Discounts: 1st class free
Notes:_____

Karate Center
Classes offered: martial arts
Location: 9 Rundlett Way,
Middleton
Major Routes/Cross Streets:
Rt.1/Rt.114
Phone: 978-777-8376
Parking: parking lot
Ages: 4-13
Website: www.thekaratecenter.com
Available for parties: n/a
Discounts: n/a
Notes:_____

Eye of the Tiger Karate Inc.
Classes offered: martial arts
Location: 600 Loring Ave., Salem
Major Routes/Cross Streets:
Vinnin Square
Phone: 978-744-5300
Parking: parking lot
Ages: 4-14

Website:
www.eyeofthetigerkarate.com
Available for parties: n/a
Discounts: n/a
Notes:_____

United Shaolin Kempo Karate
Classes offered: martial arts
Location: 43 Main St., Peabody
Major Routes/Cross Streets:
Rt.128/Main Street
Phone: 978-531-9683
Parking: parking lot
Ages: 4-14
Website:
www.unitedshaolinkempo.com
Available for parties: n/a
Discounts: n/a
Notes:_____

Choson Taekwando
Classes offered: taekwando,
kickboxing and yoga.
Location: Rte. 20, Northboro
Major Routes/Cross Streets: Rt.
20
Phone: 508-393-6900
Parking: parking lot

Ages: 4-14
Website: www.chosontkd.com
Available for parties: n/a
Discounts: n/a
Notes:_____

Karate for kids Taekwondo USA
Classes offered: martial arts
Location: 200 Great Rd., Bedford
Major Routes/Cross Streets:
Rt.225
Phone: 781-275-5362
Parking: parking lot
Ages: 4-14
Website:
www.karateforkids.tripod.com
Available for parties: n/a
Discounts: n/a
Notes:_____

Tokyo Joe's Studio Of Self Defense
Classes offered: martial arts
Location: 77 Turnpike Rd. #1b,
Ipswich
Major Routes/Cross Streets: Rt.1
Phone: 978-356-9800
Parking: parking lot

Ages: 3-14
Website: www.tokyojoesipswich.com
Available for parties: n/a
Discounts: mini karate program
Notes:_____

T Rose's Karate School
Classes offered: martial arts
Location: 386 W. Main St.,
Northboro
Major Routes/Cross Streets: Rt.20
Phone: 508-393-8779
Parking: parking lot
Ages: 5-14
Website: www.trosekarate.com
Available for parties: n/a
Discounts: n/a
Notes:_____

Holliston Bu-Ke-DO Martial Arts
Classes offered: martial arts
Location: 65 Charles St., Holliston
Major Routes/Cross Streets:
Rt.16/Hollis Street
Phone: 508-429-6688
Parking: parking lot
Ages: 5-14
Website: www.bukedo.com
Available for parties: n/a
Discounts: n/a
Notes:_____

Nick Cerio's Kempo Karate
Classes offered: martial arts
Location: 885 Waverly St.,
Framingham
Major Routes/Cross Streets:
Rt.135
Phone: 508-879-6494
Parking: parking lot
Ages: 4-14
Website: www.nickceriokenpo.com
Available for parties: n/a
Discounts: n/a
Notes:_____

Starling Taekwon-Do Academy
Classes offered: martial arts
Location: 855 Worcester Rd., Framingham
Major Routes/Cross Streets: Rt.9
Phone: 508-620-2556
Parking: parking lot
Ages: 5-14
Website: www.webpages.charter.net/mastermas
Available for parties: n/a
Discounts: n/a
Notes:_____

Villari's of Milford
Classes offered: martial arts
Location: 125 Medway Road, Milford (in Perfect Shape Gym)
Major Routes/Cross Streets: Rt.109
Phone: 508-482-0876
Parking: parking lot
Ages: 3-14
Website: www.villarisofmilford.com
Available for parties: n/a
Discounts: n/a

Notes:_____

World Class Karate & Self-defense
Classes offered: martial arts
Location: 449 Boston Post Road E, Marlboro
Major Routes/Cross Streets: Rt.2
Phone: 508-229-2545
Parking: parking lot
Ages: 4-14
Website: www.worldclasskarate.com
Available for parties: n/a
Discounts: n/a
Notes:_____

Family Karate Center
Classes offered: martial arts
Location: 116 Church St., Whitinsville
Major Routes/Cross Streets: Rt.122
Phone: 508-234-0900
Parking: parking lot
Ages: 3-14
Website: www.family-karate.com
Available for parties: n/a
Discounts: sibling discounts
Notes:_____

Family Karate Center
Classes offered: martial arts
Location: 166 Grove St., Franklin
Major Routes/Cross Streets:
Rt.495/King Street
Phone: 508-520-3807
Parking: parking lot
Ages: 3-14
Website: www.family-karate.com
Available for parties: n/a
Discounts: sibling discounts
Notes:_____

Metrowest Taekwon-do
Classes offered: martial arts
Location: 796 Boston Post Road,
Unit B-3, Marlboro
Major Routes/Cross Streets: Rt. 2
Phone: 508-624-9996
Parking: parking lot
Ages: 4-14
Website: www.metrowest-tkd.com
Available for parties: n/a
Discounts: n/a
Notes:_____

Nick Cerios Kempo Karate
Classes offered: martial arts
Location: 547 Main St., Walpole
Major Routes/Cross Streets: Rt.1A
Phone: 508-660-3997
Parking: parking lot
Ages: 4-14
Website: www.masterseavey.com
Available for parties: n/a
Discounts: n/a
Notes:_____

Nick Cerios Kempo Karate
Classes offered: martial arts
Location: 2 Man Mar Drive, Plainville
Major Routes/Cross Streets: Rt.106/Rt.152
Phone: 508-695-9178
Parking: parking lot
Ages: 4-14
Website: www.nckofplainville.com
Available for parties: n/a
Discounts: n/a
Notes:_____

Personal Best Sport Karate Center
Classes offered: martial arts
Location: 36 Commercial Street, Foxboro
Major Routes/Cross Streets: Rt.140
Phone: 508-543-1858
Parking: parking lot
Ages: 3-14
Website: www.personalbestkarate.com
Available for parties: n/a
Discounts: n/a
Notes:_____

Personal Best Sport Karate Center
Classes offered: martial arts
Location: 594 Washington Street, Easton
Major Routes/Cross Streets: Rt.138
Phone: 508-238-8333
Parking: parking lot
Ages: 3-14
Website: www.personalbestkarate.com

Available for parties: no
Discounts: n/a
Notes:_____

Personal Best Sport Karate Center
Classes offered: martial arts
Location: 250 East Main Street, Norton
Major Routes/Cross Streets: Rt.123
Phone: 508-285-5425
Parking: parking lot
Ages: 3-14
Website: www.personalbestkarate.com
Available for parties: no
Discounts: n/a
Notes:_____

Eclectic Karate
Classes offered: martial arts
Location: 11 West Main Street, Norton
Major Routes/Cross Streets: Rt.123
Phone: 508-285-7574
Parking: parking area
Ages: pre-school -14

Website: www.eclectickarate.com
Available for parties: no
Discounts: n/a
Notes:_____

Eclectic Karate
Classes offered: martial arts
Location: 160 Summer St., Kingston
Major Routes/Cross Streets: Rt.3A
Phone: 781-582-9507
Parking: parking area
Ages: pre-school -14
Website: www.eclectickarate.com
Available for parties: no
Discounts: n/a
Notes:_____

Eclectic Karate
Classes offered: martial arts
Location: 67 Everette Street, Middleboro
Major Routes/Cross Streets: Rt.495/Rt.44
Phone: 508-947-2269
Parking: parking area
Ages: pre-school - 14
Website: www.eclectickarate.com

Available for parties: no
Discounts: n/a
Notes:_____

Eclectic Karate
Classes offered: martial arts
Location: 689 Depot Street, Easton
5 Corners, Easton
Major Routes/Cross Streets:
Rt.123
Phone: 508-230-8599
Parking: parking area
Ages: pre-school -14
Website: www.eclectickarate.com
Available for parties: no
Discounts: n/a
Notes:_____

Eclectic Karate
Classes offered: martial arts
Location: 770 Broadway, Raynham
Major Routes/Cross Streets:
Rt.138
Phone: 508-880-8866
Parking: parking area
Ages: pre-school -14
Website: www.eclectickarate.com
Available for parties: no

Discounts: n/a
Notes:_____

Eclectic Karate
Classes offered: martial arts
Location: 12 West Center Street, West Bridgewater
Major Routes/Cross Streets: Rt.106
Phone: 508-588-2345
Parking: parking area
Ages: pre-school -14
Website: www.eclectickarate.com
Available for parties: no
Discounts: n/a
Notes:_____

Peter McRae's Uechi Karate
Classes offered: martial arts
Location: 95 Sandwich St., Plymouth
Major Routes/Cross Streets: Rt.3/Plimoth Plantation Highway
Phone: 508-747-2969
Parking: parking lot
Ages: 5.5-14
Website: www.okikukai.net
Available for parties: n/a

Discounts: family membership available
Notes:_____

Jade Forest Kung-Fu
Classes offered: martial arts
Location: 344 Union St., Rockland
Major Routes/Cross Streets: Rt.3A
Phone: 781-871-9062
Parking: parking lot
Ages: 4-14
Website: www.jfkungfu.com
Available for parties: n/a
Discounts: n/a
Notes:_____

Jade Forest Kung-Fu
Classes offered: martial arts
Location: 130 King Street, Cohasset (located in the back of Johnathon Livingston Plaza)
Major Routes/Cross Streets: Rt.3A/Pond Street
Phone: 781-383-6822
Parking: parking lot
Ages: 4-14
Website: www.jfkungfu.com
Available for parties: n/a

Discounts: n/a
Notes:_____

Mr. C's Kenpo Karate
Classes offered: martial arts
Location: 650 Plymouth St. #15r, East Bridgewater
Major Routes/Cross Streets: Rt.18/Central Street
Phone: 508-378-3678
Parking: parking lot
Ages: 5-14 generally
Website: www.ckka.homestead.com/ckka.html
Available for parties: n/a
Discounts: family/group discounts available
Notes:_____

Boston Tae Kwon DO
Classes offered: martial arts
Location: 1501 Bedford St. Fl 1, Abington
Major Routes/Cross Streets: Rt.18
Phone: 781-982-0400
Parking: parking lot
Ages: 3-14

Website:
www.kickboxing.com/bostonteakwo
ndo
Available for parties: n/a
Discounts: n/a
Notes:_____

American Kenpo Karate Academy
Classes offered: martial arts
Location: 170 Middle Street,
Weymouth
Major Routes/Cross Streets:
Rt.58/Main Street/ School Street
Phone: 781-331-8008
Parking: parking lot
Ages: 5-14
Website: www.akka.com
Available for parties: n/a
Discounts: web coupon
Notes:_____

American Kenpo Karate Academy
Classes offered: martial arts
Location: 6 Main Street, Hanson
Major Routes/Cross Streets: Rt.27
Phone: 781-294-4240
Parking: parking lot
Ages: 5-14

Website: www.akka.com
Available for parties: n/a
Discounts: web coupon
Notes:_____

Bridgewater Martial Arts Center
Classes offered: martial arts
Location: 27 Perkins St., Bridgewater
Major Routes/Cross Streets: Rt.18
Phone: 508-697-4947
Parking: parking lot
Ages: call (generally 4+)
Website: www.nekick.homestead.com/bmac.html
Available for parties: n/a
Discounts: n/a
Notes:_____

Martial Arts Center
Classes offered: martial arts
Location: 119 Hancock St., Braintree
Major Routes/Cross Streets: Rt.37
Phone: 781-848-5775
Parking: parking lot
Ages: 4-14

Website:
www.designfraud.com/martialartsn
ewengland/page2.html
Available for parties: n/a
Discounts: website promotion
Notes:_____

Martial Arts Center
Classes offered: martial arts
Location: 447 Turnpike Street,
Easton
Major Routes/Cross Streets:
Rt.138/West Street
Phone: 508-238-6040
Parking: parking lot
Ages: 4-14
Website:
www.designfraud.com/martialartsn
ewengland/page2.html
Available for parties: n/a
Discounts: website promotion
Notes:_____

Fred Villari's Studios
Classes offered: martial arts
Location: 58 Center St., Middleboro
Major Routes/Cross Streets:
Rt.44/Erica Avenue

Phone: 508-947-0899
Parking: parking lot
Ages: call (generally 4+)
Website: www.villari.net
Available for parties: n/a
Discounts: yes
Notes:_____

Sports/Ice Skating (including Hockey and Figure Skating)

Northern Suburbs

Chelmsford Forum
Central Mass Skating School
Classes offered: Group figure skating lessons, hockey, learn to skate
Location: 2 Brick Kiln Road, Chelmsford
Major Routes/Cross Streets:
Phone: 508-583-6804
Parking: parking lot
Ages: 3+
Website: www.fmcarenas.com
Available for parties: yes
Discounts: n/a
Notes:_____

O'Brien Rink
Classes offered: skating lessons
Location:55 Locust St #3, Woburn
Major Routes/Cross Streets:
Rt.3/Lexington Street
Phone: 781-938-1620
Parking: parking lot

Ages: 4-14
Website:
www.edgeworksskating.com
Available for parties: n/a
Discounts: n/a
Notes:_____

<u>Janas Memorial Skating Rink</u>
Classes offered: skating, hockey
Location: 415 Douglas Road, Lowell
Major Routes/Cross Streets:
Rt.495/Rt.38
Phone: 978-454-6662
Parking: parking lot
Ages: call
Website:
www.grafrink.com/janas/janas.htm
Available for parties: n/a
Discounts: n/a
Notes:_____

<u>Burlington Ice Palace</u>
Classes offered: Group figure
skating lessons, hockey, learn to
skate
Location: 36 Ray Avenue,
Burlington

Major Routes/Cross Streets:
Rt.3/Bedford Road
Phone: 781-272-9517
Parking: parking lot
Ages: 3+
Website: www.fmcarenas.com
Available for parties: yes
Discounts: n/a
Notes:_____

Navin Skating Arena
Classes offered: Group figure skating lessons, hockey, learn to skate
Location: 451 Bolton Street, Marlboro
Major Routes/Cross Streets: Rt.85
Phone: 508-624-5580
Parking: parking lot
Ages: 3+
Website: www.fmcarenas.com
Available for parties: yes
Discounts: n/a
Notes:_____

Vetran's Arena
Classes offered: Group figure skating lessons, hockey, learn to skate
Location: Panther Way, Franklin
Major Routes/Cross Streets: Rt.140
Phone: 508-541-7024
Parking: parking lot
Ages: 3+

Website: www.fmcarenas.com
Available for parties: yes
Discounts: n/a
Notes:_____

North Star Youth Forum
Central Mass Skating School
Classes offered: figure skating, hockey
Location: 15 Bridal Lane, Westboro
Major Routes/Cross Streets:
Rt.9/Oak Street
Phone: 508-366-9373
Parking: parking lot
Ages: 4-14
Website: www.nsyf.org or
www.iskatecmss.com
Available for parties: n/a
Discounts: family discount and
multiple sessions discounts
Notes: _private lessons available

Veteran's Memorial Rink
Bay State Ice Skating School
(MDC Rink)
Classes offered: skating lessons
beginner to advanced

Location: 359 Totten Pond Road, Waltham
Major Routes/Cross Streets: Rt.128
Phone: 781-890-8480
Parking: parking lot
Ages: 5-14
Website: www.iceskatingclasses.com
Available for parties: n/a
Discounts: n/a
Notes:_____

West Suburban Skating Arena
Classes offered: ice skating
Location: 35 Windsor Ave, Natick
Major Routes/Cross Streets: Rt.9/Rt.27
Phone: 508-655-1014
Parking: parking lot
Ages: 3-14
Website: www.westsuburbanarena.com
Available for parties: n/a
Discounts: n/a
Notes:_____

Babson Skating Center
Classes offered: skating classes
Location: 650 Great Plain Avenue, Wellelsey
Major Routes/Cross Streets: Rt.135
Phone: 781-239-6058
Parking: parking lot
Ages: 4.5-14
Website: see www.babson.edu
Available for parties: n/a
Discounts: n/a
Notes:_____

New England Sports Center
Classes offered: ice skating, hockey
Location: 121 Donald Lynch Blvd, Marlboro
Major Routes/Cross Streets: Rt.495/Rt.290
Phone: 508-229-2700
Parking: parking lot
Ages: call
Website: www.nes.com
Available for parties: ice available for rental
Discounts: n/a

Notes: parent/child stick time
too!

Shea Memorial Park
Bay State Ice Skating School
(MDC Rink)
Classes offered: skating lessons beginner to advanced
Location: Willard Street, Quincy
Major Routes/Cross Streets: Rt.93/Rt.137
Phone: 617-472-9325
Parking: parking lot
Ages: 5-14
Website: www.iceskatingclasses.com
Available for parties: n/a
Discounts: n/a
Notes:_____

Hetland Skating Arena
Classes offered: Group figure skating lessons, hockey, learn to skate
Location: 310 Hathaway Boulevard, New Bedford
Major Routes/Cross Streets: Rt.6/Rockdale Avenue
Phone: 508-999-9051

Parking: parking lot
Ages: 3+
Website: www.fmcarenas.com
Available for parties: yes
Discounts: n/a
Notes:_____

Armstrong Skating Arena
Classes offered: Group figure skating lessons, hockey, learn to skate
Location: Long Pond Road, Plymouth
Major Routes/Cross Streets: Rt.3/Clark Road
Phone: 508-746-8825
Parking: parking lot
Ages: 3+
Website: www.fmcarenas.com
Available for parties: yes
Discounts: n/a
Notes:_____

O'Connell Rink
Bay State Ice Skating School
(MDC Rink)
Classes offered: skating lessons beginner to advanced
Location: 220-R Broad Street, Weymouth
Major Routes/Cross Streets: Rt.3/Rt.18/Rt.53
Phone: 781-890-8480
Parking: parking lot
Ages: 5-14
Website: www.iceskatingclasses.com
Available for parties: n/a
Discounts: n/a

Alexio Skating Arena
Classes offered: Group figure skating lessons, hockey, learn to skate
Location: Gordon Owen Riverway, Taunton
Major Routes/Cross Streets: Rt.24/Rt.44
Phone: 508-824-4987
Parking: parking lot

Ages: 3+
Website: www.fmcarenas.com
Available for parties: yes
Discounts: n/a
Notes:_____

Pilgrim Skating Arena Inc
Classes offered: hockey, ice skating
Location: 75 Recreation Park Drive,
Hingham
Major Routes/Cross Streets:
Rt.53/Derby Street
Phone:781-749-6660
Parking: parking lot
Ages: hockey 4+, skating, 3+
Website: www.skatepilgrim.com
Available for parties: yes
Discounts: n/a
Notes:_____

Rockland Rink
Classes offered: skating, hockey,
figure skating
Location: 599 Summer St.,
Rockland
Major Routes/Cross Streets:
Rt.139/Concord Street
Phone: 781-878-5591

Parking: parking lot
Ages: 2-14
Website: www.ssws.com
Available for parties: yes
Discounts: n/a
Notes: _summer hockey camps

Bridgewater Ice Arena
Classes offered: skating, hockey
Location: 20 Bedford Park, Bridgewater
Major Routes/Cross Streets: Rt.24/Rt.104
Phone: 508-279-0600
Parking: parking lot
Ages: 3-14
Website: www.skatebia.com
Available for parties: yes
Discounts: n/a
Notes:_____

Driscoll Skating Arena
Classes offered: Group figure skating lessons, hockey, learn to skate
Location: 272 Ellsbree Street, Fall River
Major Routes/Cross Streets: Rt.24

Phone: 508-679-3274
Parking: parking lot
Ages: 3+
Website: www.fmcarenas.com
Available for parties: yes
Discounts: n/a
Notes:_____

Asiaf Skating Arena
Classes offered: Group figure skating lessons, hockey, learn to skate
Location: Forrest Avenue Extension, Brockton
Major Routes/Cross Streets: Rt.123/Warren Avenue
Phone: 508-583-6804
Parking: parking lot
Ages: 3+
Website: www.fmcarenas.com
Available for parties: yes
Discounts: n/a
Notes:_____

Archery USA
Classes offered: Archery classes
Location: Route 1, Dedham (Papa Gino's Plaza)
Major Routes/Cross Streets: Rt.1
Phone: 781-320-3606
Parking: parking lot
Ages: 8 and up
Website: www.archeryusa.com
Available for parties: yes
Discounts: see below
Notes: Sunday family discounts

_____

United Archery Lanes
Classes offered: archery
Location: 305 Union St., Franklin
Major Routes/Cross Streets: Rt.140
Phone: 508-520-3562
Parking: parking lot
Ages: call
Website: none
Available for parties: n/a
Discounts: n/a
Notes:_____

Archer's Lane
Classes offered: archery
Location: 11 Washington St.,
Attleboro
Major Routes/Cross Streets:
Rt.123
Phone: 508-399-6762
Parking: parking lot
Ages: call
Website: www.archerslane.com
Available for parties: yes
Discounts: n/a
Notes: available for scout group
outings too.

Nashoba Valley Ski Area
Classes offered: skiing, snowboarding
Location: 79 Powers Road, Westford
Major Routes/Cross Streets: Rt.495/Rt.110
Phone: 978-692-3033
Parking: free parking in lot
Ages: skiing from age 4, snowboarding from age 8
Website: www.skinashoba.com
Available for parties: n/a
Discounts: n/a
Notes: tubing park too for ages 6+

Wachusett Mountain Ski Area
Classes offered: skiing, snowboarding
Location: 499 Mountain Road, Princeton
Major Routes/Cross Streets: Rt.62
Phone: 978-464-2300
Parking: parking lot
Ages: 4-12
Website: www.wachusett.com

Available for parties: n/a
Discounts: n/a
Notes: _school vacation camps too_____

Blue Hill Ski Area
Classes offered: skiing, snowboarding
Location: 4001 Washington St., Canton
Major Routes/Cross Streets: Rt.93/128/Rt.138
Phone: 781-828-5070
Parking: parking lot
Ages: 7-14
Website: www.thenewbluehills.com
Available for parties: n/a
Discounts: n/a
Notes: _ski/snowboard camps too

_____

Ward Ski Area
Classes offered: skiing, snowboarding
Location: 1000 Main St., Shrewsbury
Major Routes/Cross Streets: Rt.9/South Street

Phone: 508-842-6346
Parking: parking lot
Ages: call
Website: www.skiward.com
Available for parties: n/a
Discounts: n/a
Notes: _tubing park too for ages 6+_

Guard Up
Classes offered: Fencing
Location: 16 Garfield Circle, Burlington
Major Routes/Cross Streets: I95, Exit 32B
Phone: 781-270-4800
Parking: free parking in lot (small lot) or street
Ages: 6+
Website: www.guardup.com
Available for parties: YES
Discounts: n/a
Notes: "Dragon Quest" Birthday parties and camps for martial arts too

Boston Fencing Club/Academy of Fencing
Classes offered: Fencing
Location: 110-2 Clematis Ave., Waltham
Major Routes/Cross Streets:I95 (128), Trapelo Road
Phone: 781-891-0119
Parking: parking lot

Ages: 5-14
Website:
www.bostonfencingclub.org
Available for parties: n/a
Discounts: n/a
Notes:_____

Cohasset Sailing Club
Classes offered: sailing lessons
Location: 19 Lighthouse Lane,
Cohasset
Major Routes/Cross Streets:
Rt.3A/Gannet Road/Border Street
Phone: 781-383-1513
Parking: free parking with beach
sticker
Ages: 10+
Website:
www.cohassetsailingclub.com
Available for parties: n/a
Discounts: n/a
Notes:_____

City of Lawrence/Lawrence
Recreation Department
Classes offered: sailing and boating
instruction
Location: 200 Common St.,
Lawrence
Major Routes/Cross Streets: Rt.
93/Eaton Street.
Phone: 978-681-8675
Parking: free parking in lot

Ages: call
Website: n/a
Available for parties: no
Discounts: n/a
Notes: <u>classes held at Lawrence Riverfront State Park</u>

Skater's Paradise
Classes offered: skateboarding
Location: 590 Lake Street,
Shrewsbury
Major Routes/Cross Streets:
Rt.495/Rt.9/Rt.20
Phone: 508-757-1115
Parking: parking lot
Ages: all ages
Website: www.skaterparadise1.com
Available for parties: yes
Discounts: n/a
Notes: summer skateboard
clinics

Skater's Paradise
Classes offered: skateboarding
Location: 92 Blandin Avenue,
Framingham
Major Routes/Cross Streets:
Rt.30/Rt.135
Phone: 508-665-5012
Parking: parking lot
Ages: all ages
Website: www.skaterparadise1.com
Available for parties: yes

Discounts: n/a
Notes: summer skateboard clinics_____

RAMpage Skate Park/Sk8palace
Classes offered: skateboarding
Location: 110 South Main Street, Milford
Major Routes/Cross Streets: Rt.495/Rt.85/Rt.16
Phone: 508-473-6611
Parking: parking lot
Ages: all ages
Website: www.sk8palace.com
Available for parties: yes
Discounts: n/a
Notes: after-school skateboard lessons_____

Theater

Northern Suburbs

Concord Youth Theater
Classes offered: Drama classes including: Story theater, Monsters Magic & Make Believe, Musical theater, Kids company, and performance workshops.
Location: 40 Stow St., Concord
Major Routes/Cross Streets: Rt.126/Sudbury Road
Phone: 978-371-1482
Parking: parking lot and street parking
Ages: 3-14
Website: www.concordyouththeater.org
Available for parties: N/A
Discounts: N/A
Notes: auditions open to ages 9 and above

Kidstock Creative Theater Education Center

Classes offered: workshops in creative theater, video production and studio art.
Location: 50 Cross St., Winchester (Artspace at the Mill)
Major Routes/Cross Streets: Rt.38
Phone: 781-729-5543
Parking: parking lot
Ages: 4-14
Website: www.kidstocktheater.com
Available for parties: YES
Discounts: n/a
Notes: School vacation programs available.

Neverland Theater

Classes offered: drama classes
Location: First Methodist Church 391 Bay Road, Hamilton – call to confirm location of classes
Major Routes/Cross Streets: Rt.1A
Phone: 978-468-1191
Parking: parking lot
Ages: 8-14
Website: www.neverlandtheater.com
Available for parties: n/a

Discounts: n/a
Notes:_____

Performing Arts Center of Metrowest

Classes offered: dramatic play, improvisition, storytelling, scene study, character work, creating a TV show, improv comedy, as well as children's theater and comedy troupes.

Location: 140 Pearl Street, Framingham

Major Routes/Cross Streets: Rt.126/Lincoln Street

Phone: 508-875-5554

Parking: free parking in lot, metered parking in street

Ages: 4-14

Website: www.framingham.com/org/mwpac.htm

Available for parties: n/a

Discounts: members

Notes: _____

Turtle Lane Children's Theater
Classes offered: theater workshops-acting, singing, dancing and stagecraft
Location: 283 Melrose Street, Auburndale
Major Routes/Cross Streets: Rt.128/95/Rt.30
Phone: 617-244-5058
Parking: parking area
Ages: call
Website: www.turtle-lane.com
Available for parties: n/a
Discounts: n/a
Notes: _check website for audition opportunities_

Steps off Broadway Theater
Classes offered:
Location: 9 Airport Drive, Hopedale
Major Routes/Cross Streets: Rt.140/Hartford Avenue/Plain Street
Phone: 508-478-7274
Parking: parking lot
Ages: 3-14
Website: www.steps-dancing.com
Available for parties: n/a

Discounts: n/a
Notes:_____

Milford Performing Arts Center
Classes offered: drama classes
Location: Memorial Hall, 30 School Street, Milford
Major Routes/Cross Streets: Rt.16/Purchase Street
Phone: 508-473-1684
Parking: parking lot
Ages: call
Website: www.milford.ma.us/mpac.htm
Available for parties: no
Discounts: n/a
Notes:_____

Franklin School of Performing Arts
Classes offered: drama classes, musical theater
Location: 38 Main St., Franklin
Major Routes/Cross Streets: Rt.140
Phone: 508-528-8668
Parking: street parking
Ages: 6-14

Website: www.FSPAonline.com
Available for parties: no
Discounts: some
Notes: vacation and summer programs too___

The Un-common Theater Company
Classes offered: none- auditions only
Location: 71 Mill Street, Mansfield
Major Routes/Cross Streets: Rt.106
Phone: 508-339-0037
Parking: parking area
Ages: depending on role
Website: www.uncommontheater.com
Available for parties: no
Discounts: n/a
Notes:_____

Puppet Showplace Theatre

Classes offered: theater workshops and summer camp
Location: 32 Station St., Brookline
Major Routes/Cross Streets: Rt.128/Washington Street/Station Street (across from T station)
Phone: 617-731-6400
Parking: street parking
Ages: Grades 4-9
Website: www.puppetshowplace.org
Available for parties: yes
Discounts: n/a
Notes: school vacation programs too

All Newton Music School Inc.

Classes offered: musical theater
Location: 321 Chestnut St., West Newton
Phone: 617-527-4553
Major Routes/Cross Streets: Rt.90/Rt.16
Parking: very limited parking in lot
Ages: call
Website: www.newtonarts.com/id11.htm
Available for parties: no
Discounts: in some cases

Notes:_____

Telamon Community Center
Classes offered: introduction to theatre and dramatic arts classes
Location: 14 School St., Medway
Major Routes/Cross Streets: Rt.109/Village Street
Phone: 508-533-2400
Parking: parking lot
Ages: 6-13
Website: www.telamonctr.com
Available for parties: no
Discounts: members
Notes:_____

Stage Door Dance Theater
Classes offered: voice lessons
Location: 796 Boston Post Road East, Marlboro
Major Routes/Cross Streets: Rt.20
Phone: 508-786-0350
Parking: parking lot
Ages: call
Website: www.stagedoordance.com
Available for parties: no
Discounts: multiple class discounts
Notes:_____

Southern Suburbs

Fiddlehead Theater
Classes offered: drama, theater
Location: 109 Central Street, Norwood
Major Routes/Cross Streets: Rt.1/Nahatan Street
Phone: 781-762-4060
Parking: street parking, public lots
Ages: 7-14
Website: www.fiddleheadtheater.com
Available for parties: n/a
Discounts: n/a
Notes:_____

Summer Stage
Classes offered: theater workshops-auditioning, movement, mime, improvisation, stage make-up, puppetry, Shakespeare, character development and more
Location: 1186 Washington Street, South Walpole (in the South Walpole Methodist Church)

Major Routes/Cross Streets:
Rt.95/Rt.1
Phone: 781-278-9745
Parking: parking lot
Ages: 7-14
Website: www.summerdrama.com
Available for parties: no
Discounts: family discounts
available
Notes:_____

The Walpole Children's Theater
Classes offered: none-auditions
only. Children's theater performed
by children.
Location: Walpole –call for location
of production
Major Routes/Cross Streets:
Rt.95/Rt.1
Phone: 508-668-5499
Parking: parking lot or street
parking
Ages: call
Website:
www.homestead.com/WalpoleChildr
ensTheater1/wcthomepage.html
Available for parties: n/a
Discounts: n/a

Notes: call for performance, audition and rehearsal locations

The Orpheum Theater
Classes offered: acting, theater, improve, theater technology
Location: on Foxboro common, Foxboro
Major Routes/Cross Streets: Rt.95/Mechanic Street
Phone: 508-543-4434
Parking: street parking and public lots
Ages: 5-14
Website: www.orpheum.org
Available for parties: n/a
Discounts: n/a
Notes:_____

APPENDICES

ALPHABETICAL INDEX BY LISTING

C

Drumlin Farm Education Center and Wildlife Sanctuary (70,218)
Duval Dance Studio (176)

E
East Coast Golf Academy (266)
Eclectic Karate-Norton (291)
Eclectic Karate-Kingston (292)
Eclectic Karate-Middleboro (292)
Eclectic Karate-Easton (293)
Eclectic Karate-Raynham (293)
Eclectic Karate-West Bridgewater (294)
Edaville Railroad (17)
Ellen's School of Dance-Billerica (150)
Ellen's School of Dance-Burlington (150)
Ellen's School of Dance-Tyngsboro (151)
Endicott Park (107)
Essex Shipbuilding Museum (41)
European School of Music (192)
Exxcel (250)
Eye of the Tiger Karate (281)

F

Family Karate Center-Whitinsville (287)
Family Karate Center-Franklin (288)
Fiddlehead Theater (335)
Flipside Gymnastics (253)
Fontaine Academy of Dance (174)
Franklin School of Performing Arts (125, 155, 198, 207,331)
Fred Villari's Studios (299)
French for Kids (181)
Fuller Museum of Art (53,132)

G

Garden in the Woods (77,221)
Golf Teaching Center (265)
Grace Chapel School of Creative Arts (189)
Great Brook Farm State Park (110)
Great Meadows Natural Wildlife Sanctuary (79)
Guard Up! (228,320)
Gymboree-Burlington (245)
Gymboree-Plymouth (213,260)
Gymboree-Westboro (231)
Gymnastics & More (243)
Gymnastic Academy of Boston (258)
Gymnastics Express (256)

Gymnastic Learning Center (246)
Gymnastics Training Center (252)

H
Habitat Education Center and
Wildlife Sanctuary (65,220)
Habitat for Soccer & Sports (230)
Halifax Music (213)
Hamilton-Wenham School of Dance
(145)
Hammond Castle Museum (40)
Harold Parker State Forest (109)
Harvard Ridge Pool Club (233)
Head Over Heels Gymnastics Inc.
(260)
Hetland Skating Arena (309)
Holliston Bu-ke-Do Martial Arts
(285)
Honeypot Hill Orchards (92)
Hopkinton State Park (115)
Horrigan Drum School (215)
House of 7 Gables (24)
Hull Lifesaving museum (56)
Hyland Orchards and Brewery (94)

I
Indian Hill Music Center (197)
Ipswich River (219)

Kerry Smith's Academy of Dance Arts (179)
Kidstock Creative Theater Education Center (327)

L

Laurene Aldorisio Academy of Dance Expression (156)
Le Studio Danse (161)
Let's Dance Inc. (149)
Lexington Arts and Crafts Society (123)
Lil Folk Farm (76)
Longfellow Sports Club (230,235)
Lynn Shore Reservation/Nahant Beach (104)
Lynn Woods Reservation (106)

M

Marblehead School of Ballet (140)
Martial Arts Center-Easton (299)
Martial Arts Center-Braintree (298)
Marie Austin School of Dance (178)
Marine Museum at Fall River (62)
Marino Lookout Farm (74, 95)
Massachusetts Gymnastics Center – Hingham (257)

Music Together-Medway (199)
Music Together-Hopedale (210)
Music Together-Newton (211)
Museum of Transportation (50)

N
Nancy Kelley Dance Studio (165)
Nashoba Valley Ski Area (317)
Nashoba Valley Winery &
Orchards (90)
Natick Community Organic
Farm (75)
Natick Racquet Club (273)
Navin Skating Arena (304)
Needham Dance Theater (164)
Needham Music (202)
Neverland Theater (327)
New Arts Center in Newton (129)
New Bedford Whaling Museum (58)
New England Piano (206)
New England Pirate Museum (37)
New England Quilt Museum (43)
New England Sports Center (307)
New Bedford Fire Museum (63)
Newton Indoor Sports (229)
Nick Cerio's Kempo Karate-
Framingham (285)

Q

R

S

T

W

Wachusett Mountain Ski Area and State Reservation (103)
Wachusett Mountain Ski Area (317)
Walden Pond (102)
Walpole Dance Center (169)
Walpole Gymnastics Academy (257)
Waltham Athletic Club (275)
Ward's Berry Farm (101)
Ward Ski Area (318)
Wayside Racquet & Swim Club (236,274)
Westboro Tennis & Swim Club (275)
Westford Racquet & Fitness (233)
Weston Racquet Club (274)
Westward orchards (96)
West Suburban Skating Arena (306)
Weymouth Tennis Club (277)
Whistler House Museum of Art (42)
Whitehall State Park (116)
Whitinsville Golf Club (267)
Willows Racquet & Fitness Center (271)
Wimbledon 109 Tennis Club (276)
Wolf Hollow (69)
World Class Karate & Self defense (287)

Y

Yang's Andover – Martial Arts & Fitness (142)

NOTES

TOWN INDEX - OUTINGS AND ACTIVITIES

	Themed Adventure	Historic Sites	Museums	Nature & Animals	Orchards	Parks & Hiking
North Suburbs						
Acton			X			
Belmont				X		
Berlin					X	
Bolton					X	
Carlisle						X
Chelmsford						
Concord		X				X
Danvers						X
Essex			X			
Gloucester			X			
Harvard					X	
Ipswich				X	X	
Lexington		X				
Lincoln			X	X		
Lowell			X			
Lynn						X
Marblehead			X			
Princeton						X
Salem	X	X	X			
Saugus		X				X
Stow					X	
Sterling				X	X	
Stoneham				X		
Sutton						X
Wenham			X			
Westford				X		
West Suburbs						
Ashland	X					
Brookline			X			
Douglas	X					
Framingham			X	X		X
Holliston				X		
Hopkinton						X
Mendon				X		X
Natick				X		X
Norfolk				X		
South Natick					X	
Sudbury				X		
Sturbridge	X					
Waltham			X			
Weston			X			
Wrentham					X	
South Suburbs						

Attleboro				X	X		
Brockton				X			
Bridgewater						X	
Carver	X						X
Easton				X			
Fall River				X			
Hull				X			
Marshfield					X		
Milton				X	X		X
Norwell					X		
New Bedford				X			
Plymouth	X	X		X			
Quincy				X			
Sharon					X	X	

TOWN INDEX-CLASSES

North Suburbs	Art	Dance	Language	Music	Nature & Science	Sports	Theater
Acton				x		x	
Amesbury		x		x			
Andover	x			x			
Bedford				x		x	
Belmont		x			x		
Berlin						x	
Beverly		x	x	x			
Billerica		x					
Bolton							
Boxborough						x	
Bradford				x		x	
Burlington		x				x	
Carlisle							
Chelmsford		x				x	
Concord				x		x	x
Danvers		x					
Essex							
Georgetown						x	
Gloucester		x		x			
Hamilton		x					x
Harvard							
Haverhill	x	x		x			
Ipswich						x	
Lawrence						x	
Lexington	x	x	x	x		x	
Lincoln					x		
Littleton				x			
Lowell						x	
Lynn							
Marblehead		x		x			
Middleton		x				x	
Newburyport					x		
North Andover		x		x		x	
North Billerica						x	
North Reading		x		x			
Peabody		x		x		x	
Princeton						x	
Reading		x				x	
Salem		x				x	
Saugus							
Stow							
Sterling							
Stoneham		x					
Sutton							
Tewksbury		x					
Topsfield					x		
Tyngsboro		x				x	

Wakefield				x		x	
Wenham						x	
Westford		x				x	
Winchester		x	x	x			x
Woburn				x		x	
West Suburbs							
Ashland		x				x	
Auburndale							x
Bellingham						x	
Brookline							x
Chestnut Hill			x				
Dover		x					
Framingham	x	x		x	x	x	x
Franklin	x	x		x		x	x
Grafton				x			
Holliston		x		x		x	
Hopedale				x		x	x
Hopkinton	x	x				x	
Marlboro		x				x	x
Medfield		x					
Medway	x			x		x	x
Mendon						x	
Milford				x		x	x
Millis	x	x					
Natick				x	x	x	
Needham	x	x		x		x	
Needham Heights	x						
Newton	x	x	x	x		x	x
North Grafton		x					
Norfolk					x		
Northboro		x	x			x	
Shrewsbury				x		x	
Southboro	x						
South Natick							
Sudbury						x	
Sturbridge							
Upton		x					
Uxbridge						x	
Waltham		x		x		x	
Wellesley			x			x	
Westboro	x	x		x		x	
Weston				x			
Whitinsville						x	

South Suburbs							
Abington						X	
Attleboro					X	X	
Braintree		X			X	X	
Brockton	X	X		X		X	
Bridgewater		X			X	X	
Canton					X	X	
Carver							
Cohasset						X	
Dedham						X	
Duxbury		X		X			
Easton						X	
East Bridgewater						X	
Fall River						X	
Foxboro		X				X	X
Halifax		X		X			
Hanover		X					
Hanson		X				X	
Hingham				X		X	
Holbrook						X	
Hull							
Kingston				X			
Lakeville		X					
Marshfield					X		
Mansfield	X	X					X
Middleboro						X	
Milton							
Norwell					X	X	
Norwood		X				X	X
North Attleboro						X	
North Dartmouth						X	
Norton						X	
New Bedford						X	
Pembroke		X		X			
Plainville						X	
Plymouth						X	
Quincy						X	
Raynham		X				X	
Rockland		X				X	
Scituate		X					
Sharon					X		
Stoughton				X		X	
Taunton						X	
Walpole	X	X				X	X
West Bridgewater						X	
Weymouth				X			
Whitman						X	

ORDER FORM

Please use this form to order additional copies or new yearly editions.

Name:_____

Mailing address:_____

City:_____

State:_____Zip Code:_____

Telephone Number:_____

Email:_____

Title	Number of copies	Price per copy	Total
		$19.95	
		Shipping	$4.00
		Additional Shipping*	
		Tax MA5%	
		Order total	

*add $2 for each additional book

TO ORDER

BY MAIL: please send this form, with payment enclosed to: Kiwi Publishing, P.O. Box 493, Hopkinton MA 01748

BY FAX: please fax this form to 508-435-0378 (*credit cards only)

BY EMAIL/WEB: please visit our website www.adventuresinsuburbia.com

Payment Method:

Check or Money Order made payable to **Kiwi Publishing**.

Credit Cards: Master Card( ) or Visa ( )
Card Number_____
Expiration Date_____
Name on Card_____

ORDER FORM

Please use this form to order additional copies or new yearly editions.

Name:_____

Mailing address:_____

City:_____

State:_____Zip Code:_____

Telephone Number:_____

Email:_____

Title	Number of copies	Price per copy	Total
		$19.95	
		Shipping	$4.00
		Additional Shipping*	
		Tax MA5%	
		Order total	

*add $2 for each additional book

TO ORDER

BY MAIL: please send this form, with payment enclosed to: Kiwi Publishing, P.O. Box 493, Hopkinton MA 01748

BY FAX: please fax this form to 508-435-0378 (*credit cards only)

BY EMAIL/WEB: please visit our website www.adventuresinsuburbia.com

Payment Method:

Check or Money Order made payable to **Kiwi Publishing**.

Credit Cards: Master Card( ) or Visa ( )
Card Number_____
Expiration Date_____
Name on Card_____

Adventures in Suburbia—Boston 2003

ORDER FORM

Please use this form to order additional copies or new yearly editions.

Name:_____

Mailing address:_____

City:_____

State:_____Zip Code:_____

Telephone Number:_____

Email:_____

Title	Number of copies	Price per copy	Total
		$19.95	
		Shipping	$4.00
		Additional Shipping*	
		Tax MA5%	
		Order total	

*add $2 for each additional book

TO ORDER

BY MAIL: please send this form, with payment enclosed to: Kiwi Publishing, P.O. Box 493, Hopkinton MA 01748

BY FAX: please fax this form to 508-435-0378 (*credit cards only)

BY EMAIL/WEB: please visit our website www.adventuresinsuburbia.com

Payment Method:

Check or Money Order made payable to **Kiwi Publishing**.

Credit Cards: Master Card( ) or Visa ( )
Card Number_____
Expiration Date_____
Name on Card_____